THE ENCYCLOPEDIA OF
Printmaking
TECHNIQUES

A unique visual directory of printmaking
techniques, with guidance on how to use them

Judy Martin

Search Press

A QUARTO BOOK

This edition published in 2018 by
Search Press Ltd
Wellwood
North Farm Road
Tunbridge Wells
Kent TN2 3DR
United Kingdom

Previously published by Search
Press Ltd as The Encyclopedia of
Printmaking Techniques in 2006

Copyright © 2006, 2018 Quarto
Publishing plc
An imprint of The Quarto Group

ISBN 978-1-78221-645-2

Conceived, edited and designed by
Quarto Publishing plc
The Old Brewery
6 Blundell Street
London N7 9BH

www.quartoknows.com

QUAR.EPMN

Editor: Claire Waite Brown
Design: Nick Clark
(www.fogdog.co.uk)
Senior Designer: Martina Calvio
Publisher: Samantha Warrington

Printed in China

10 9 8 7 6 5 4 3 2 1

Page 2, Vanessa Lubach Farewell to a
Norfolk Summer (detail)

Contents

Introduction

Printmaking covers an impressively wide range of activities and pictorial matter – there is something for everyone here. But printmaking studios, with their strange, alchemical combinations of unfamiliar materials, purpose-made tools and monumental machinery, can seem like alien territory, even to experienced artists quite comfortable with other kinds of studio practice.

However, there is no need to be daunted by the technicalities, because many of the printmaking processes are very straightforward and easy to grasp. Some, such as lithography and etching, are inherently more complex, but they can be learned in stages so that the newcomer can gradually build confidence and grow in ambition. In fact, the need to follow specific technical procedures provides a framework for the creative side of image-making that many artists regard as a supportive element. As you become immersed in practicalities, the process itself suggests ways of interpreting your image.

This book is an invaluable introduction to printmaking methods, taking you step by step through the technical details, as well as providing inspirational examples of prints in all media. In this book the priority is to relate the techniques and inspirational images to things you can easily achieve yourself with readily available equipment and facilities. Although it is necessary to have access to a properly equipped studio and presses in order to develop the full potential of most techniques, there are methods you can carry out from start to finish working on your kitchen or living-room table. Once you have understood the principles and mastered some basic techniques, you can bring your own inventiveness and creativity into play to adapt the chosen methods to suit your style of work and situation.

Tools and Techniques

The step-by-step demonstrations in this section of the book are the ideal introduction to the range of printmaking methods. The sequences are designed to provide a clear explanation of what the materials, tools and equipment can do in each case, and why certain procedures are necessary. Once you begin to work with your chosen method you will soon acquire the practical knowledge that enables you to think creatively in terms of printmaking itself.

Printmaking methods

There are two main reasons for choosing to produce an original image as a print, one being to obtain a number of identical copies. The motive for this may be to originate pictures as multiple images or to reinterpret an existing painting or drawing in print form. Because prints sell more cheaply than one-off originals they are accessible to people who do not normally invest in art and can thus represent a useful share of an artist's income. For the amateur, there is a considerable pleasure in having works on paper that can be sold cheaply or given to friends, while one or more can be retained by the artist.

The second reason for making prints is that each process produces characteristic visual qualities quite different from those of a directly drawn or painted image. For example, the flat, glossy colour areas you see in a linocut or silkscreen print cannot easily be obtained with paint and brush; and the grainy, integrated textures of chalk drawing and ink washes produced by lithography are distinctly different in feeling to similar marks applied directly on paper. Etching is a law unto itself: an etched line is not at all like a drawn line, and there are many ways of achieving etched textures that give an exciting variety to this medium.

The way the image is produced influences not only

the character of the finished work but the way you conceive and plan it. Before you start to consider which processes would suit you best, take account of the following basic principles.

Basic principles

The methods of producing a printed image can be divided into four main categories: relief printing, intaglio, planographic (printing from a flat surface) and stencil processes. In the relief-printing techniques of linocut, woodcut and wood engraving (pages 36–53), the original flat surface of the wood or lino block represents the printing surface. Any parts of the design not to be printed are cut away, leaving

the image raised in relief. This is usually inked with a roller, and transferred to paper by direct pressure.

Intaglio processes – drypoint, mezzotint and etching – are the opposite. These are usually done on metal plates, and the design is incised or etched into the surface. It is the sunken lines and areas of the plate that are printed, by pushing ink into them and applying heavy pressure to press the paper into the inked marks; the original surface level of an intaglio plate represents the white in a black and white image.

Lithography is a planographic process, meaning that the printing and non-printing areas

◀ **HELEN PEYTON**
FISH TV (LINOCUT)
Having to work in reverse is one of the most testing elements to reduction linocutting. Even though preparation is slow and deliberate, trying to fully plan the stages can never give a true idea of how a finished piece will look. When printing, try to let the piece develop with every ongoing cut and colour.

are on the same level. The image is drawn on a metal plate (or litho stone) and processed so that it 'sets' into the grain of the surface. Lithographic prints can be taken by direct pressure or by offsetting. On an offset press, plate and paper are placed side by side; a roller travels over the plate and picks up the inked image; on travelling back, it deposits the image on the paper.

Screenprinting is basically a stencilling process. The screen has a stretched, fine mesh which transmits an even layer of ink under pressure. To create the image, parts of the mesh must be blocked so they cannot allow the ink through. There are many different ways of preparing stencils, all of which produce characteristically different qualities in the imagery.

Negative and positive

A printed image taken by direct pressure is always reversed on the paper because the original block or plate is in face-to-face contact with it. Relief, intaglio and lithographic printing on a

▲ **CELIA LEWIS**
CHERRIES IN GREEN BOWL
(LINOCUT)
To create her linocut prints the
artist uses plates that fit together
like the pieces of a jigsaw. She
inks the separate parts, then fits
them back together and puts them
through the press in one pass.

▶ **ANITA REYNOLDS**
DAY 56 – BALLARD DOWN
(DRYPOINT)
Using drypoint on perspex
produces marks that are similar
to sketches: rapid, dynamic and
slightly unpredictable in nature.
The burr raised up by the pointed
tools, to which the ink attaches,
gives a characteristic dull, fuzzy
line that is unique to this technique
and not similar to a charcoal mark.

direct-pressure press produce
reversed images. With offset
lithography the image is put
down on the paper in the same
position as it was picked up
from the plate – there is no
direct contact between plate and
paper – so it is not reversed. In
screenprinting, too, the image is
right-reading – the ink passes
through the screen mesh rather
than being printed off from it.

This left-to-right reversal is
not the only 'opposite' element
you have to keep in mind when
preparing images for printing.
Often you are required to work
in negative – that is, the marks
you make with your printmaking
tools represent the non-printing
areas of the design. In relief
prints, the parts of the block
that you actively cut away
surround the parts that will read
as the image. In screenprinting,
where you are preparing a
stencil to print, for example,
blue areas of the image, the
stencil itself will consist of all
those areas that will not be blue.
Conversely, in lithography and
most intaglio processes, the
marks you make are those that
directly create the image.

These concepts can seem
confusing when put into words,
but they start to make sense as
you come to deal with them in
practice. There are also
exceptions to the rules – for
example, resist techniques for
preparing a screen image, and

one or two specific etching techniques, when you do invert the normal procedures. For this reason you need to start simply with any printmaking method, learning the basics that give you the ability to think through the processing in logical steps. As you gain in experience and confidence, you can discover the variations that enable you to exploit the properties of your medium more fully and apply them to an expressive rendering of your subject.

Colour and texture

Prints of the same subject carried out in the full range of media show some of the characteristic differences between printmaking processes and their effects. Monoprints and collage prints are technically quite simple to make, but can provide a wide range of painterly qualities. The intaglio methods of drypoint and mezzotint are primarily tonal, but approached differently – drypoint by drawing positively in black line and tone, mezzotint by burnishing whites out of dark texture. Similarly, wood engraving typically appears as white lines on black, while the other relief methods – woodcut and linocut – more often rely on black key-line images, although both are easily adapted to colour printing. Etching, lithography and screenprinting each incorporate a variety of techniques enabling equally varied, simple or sophisticated surface effects.

Monoprints (see page 20)

Linocut (see page 26)

Screenprinting (see page 60)

Drypoint (see page 76)

Woodcut (see page 36)

Wood engraving (see page 46)

Collage blocks (see page 54)

Mezzotint (see page 80)

Etching (see page 84)

Lithography (see page 110)

The work environment

There is no doubt that the ideal situation for learning and practising all the major printmaking processes is a properly equipped print studio. For most non-professional artists, the easiest and least expensive way to achieve this goal is to join organised classes in printmaking at a local art school or adult-education institute. For the more ambitious who would like to devote some regular time to specific processes, it may be possible to hire time in a professional studio or join a co-operative of artists sharing printmaking facilities.

However, having no access, or very limited access, to a studio by no means disqualifies you from producing interesting prints. Monoprints, linocuts, woodcuts, wood engravings and collage prints can all be prepared and printed at home. The main advantage of using a print studio is access to a printing press, which enables you to produce reliable, good-quality impressions quite quickly. But you can produce finished prints from flat surfaces and blocks by a simple hand-printing method. Alternatively, you can prepare printing blocks at home and take hand-printed proofs, then arrange to use a print studio only for the time you need to refine the design and take your final prints on the press.

Printing presses

There are various printing presses, some dedicated to one printing method, others adaptable to more than one. A relief-printing press typically relies on direct pressure. In flat-bed presses such as the Albion and Columbian types, the block is placed on the bed of the press and an upper surface is brought down to exert heavy pressure on paper and block. An alternative is the old-style type-proofing press, formerly used by typesetters. This kind of press has a sunken bed in which a thick wood or wood-mounted lino block can be set. A cylinder with the paper attached is rolled across the block under pressure.

Intaglio printing is done on a roller press, a flat, heavy metal bed suspended between two rollers. The space between the rollers is adjusted to vary the pressure, as required; the metal intaglio plate with paper laid on top is positioned on the bed, and the bed is passed between the rollers. This press can be adapted to relief printing provided that the original block is not too thick to be accommodated by the rollers. A relief-printing press, however, cannot normally be used for intaglio because it does not exert sufficient pressure to force the paper down into the sunken areas of the plate.

For offset lithography, a specialised press is required. This has a long bed on which the paper and plate are positioned side by side. A very large, heavy roller occupying the whole width

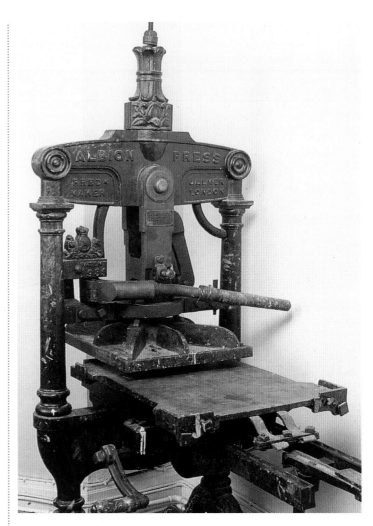

Using a flat-bed press
1 The upright section of the press supports a heavy platen that moves downwards when the bar is pulled across. The flat bed is rolled out from underneath the platen to position the block and sheet of paper, then taken back underneath before pressure is applied.

2 The handle is turned the other way to take the bed right back underneath the platen, to position the block centrally so that even pressure will be applied.

3 With the bed in position, the artist grasps the bar and pulls it towards them, which lowers the platen onto the bed. This takes some effort, since the downwards pressure activated by the movement of the bar is powerful.

of the bed trundles along its entire length, moved either by a handle or an electrically powered mechanism. The rubber 'blanket' around the roller picks up ink from the plate as it passes forwards, then puts it down on the paper as it moves back.

Large printing presses are cumbersome, heavy and extremely expensive. Even if you could find an affordable secondhand one, you might need to have the floor of your workroom strengthened to accommodate it. New roller-press models are more compact and lightweight. The capital outlay is considerable, but you will have a machine that will see service for years. On a smaller scale, table-top versions of the intaglio roller press are available at reasonable prices.

Screenprinting facilities

You can easily set up a small-scale screenprinting operation at home, since the basic equipment is self-contained, relatively lightweight and can be constructed to a required size. You must have a perfectly flat surface for printing, so it is best to hinge the screen to a permanent printing bed or baseboard so it can be raised and lowered freely. Screens can be bought ready made from some art and craft retailers, or you can make your own – there are a number of specialist publications that explain how to do this in full detail.

If you are working in a print studio, you may be using a metal printing frame attached to

Proofing press
This kind of press was originally designed for printing type blocks to produce galley proofs of texts. The bed of the press accommodates the height of the type blocks, so is ideal for printing woodcut blocks and wood-mounted lino. The paper is fitted to the cylinder, which is then rolled over the inked block.

a vacuum bed. The frame is adjustable so that the screen can be securely locked into it. The printing bed has a network of small holes across its full length and width. When the mechanism that creates the vacuum is switched on during printing, it creates suction from below that holds the paper down on the flat surface.

Work areas

The other advantage of a properly set-up studio is that there is an allotted space for each stage of the work. This helps to keep the work clean and the tools and equipment in good condition. Also, different chemicals can be stored separately to avoid accident.

Etching press
A press for printing intaglio plates, which are only a few millimetres thick. When a geared handle is turned, a flat metal bed passes between two weighty metal rollers. To soften and spread the pressure, blankets are used to cushion the action of the rollers.

If you are working at home on relief prints or screenprinting, there are a few basic guidelines to take into account. For simple, practical reasons, it is helpful to have separate areas for preparation and printing, because this allows you to work on both during one session without taking time to clear up and reorganise. For example, cutting blocks or preparing a screen stencil could be done in one area and printing off from them in another. You can also keep sharp cutting tools away from other pieces of equipment that are vulnerable to damage, such as soft gelatin rollers.

One important space that it is easy to overlook is an area where prints can be left to dry.

Metal drying racks
The metal frames form a stack, each frame hinged at the back so it can be lifted easily to slip in prints on lower layers. This kind of drying rack is highly suitable for relief prints, screenprints and lithographs.

Ceiling racks
1 These purpose-made wooden racks have slots containing a ball-and-wire mechanism that grips the top edge of the print and allows the paper to hang straight.

2 To insert the print, the ball is pushed upwards and the paper slipped in against the wire. When the ball drops back, its own weight secures the paper. The same action releases the print.

and metal-frame stacks that flap up and down so you can insert the prints to lie flat on a wire grid in several layers. Intaglio prints, which are taken on damp paper, are usually pressed between boards while drying, so that the paper does not buckle. The prints are leaved between blotting or tissue paper so they don't come into contact with each other.

Safety

Safety factors are particularly important in both etching and lithography. Various stages of etching involve working on the metal plates with heat, acid or flammable substances, while chemical preparations are used in lithography, and the flexible metal plates and mechanical press require careful management. However, under proper guidance, both processes are quite safe. Any chemical that gives off fumes must be used in an area with good ventilation, and goggles, a face mask and rubber gloves are necessary precautions when you are dealing with acid or other caustic liquids.

Generally, however, your alertness to the safety angle should be much the same as when you are cooking or carrying out home repairs. Don't leave things to 'cook' on a hotplate; don't let sharp tools lie about exposed or jumble up different types of equipment; and immediately clean up liquids or inks that spill on the floor so that you don't slip.

You may wish to print twenty or thirty impressions at one time, in which case you will have a lot of pieces of paper that have to be stored separately for up to two days – and left somewhere where they can dry flat with no risk of sticking together. A simple solution is a 'washing-line' system of cords strung above eye level, on which prints can be hung using bulldog clips or similar fastenings. If you have a plan chest, which is useful storage for clean paper and drawings or paintings as well, you can lay out the prints for drying as the top layer of each drawer. Or you can construct a wood or metal shelving system with shallow openings so that the prints can be leafed in to lie flat on the shelves.

Studio drying systems include wooden ceiling-hung racks with ball-and-wire attachments that grip the top edge of the prints,

Safety features
The acid bath in an etching studio is one of the most obviously hazardous work areas, which needs special facilities. This one sits below a ventilator hood, and can be completely enclosed by drawing down the plastic sides of the boxed-in area. The artist takes the precaution of wearing goggles and rubber gloves when working with the acid.

Producing prints

Getting from the picture in your mind's eye to the finished print on paper is not just a matter of technical skill, but also of working with the medium appropriately at each stage of processing. This includes the way you initially conceive and prepare your image for print form. For the beginner, this is a chicken-and-egg situation – if you don't know what the process can do, how can you plan the final image? On the other hand, if you haven't begun with a definite visual idea, what are you going to work on in order to learn how to print?

To find out what the particular marks and materials you apply will turn into when processed and printed, you can start off by working direct on a block, plate or screen in a purely abstract manner. A test plate or block is not an unusual first step. You probably won't achieve a finished image with much form to it in this way, but you may find you have produced a useful reference chart for future use.

Working drawings

More commonly, you will start with some reference work – a sketch, drawing, painting or photograph – as the basis for the print. The first thing to realise is that any form of printmaking is an interpretive, not a reproductive method. In other words, the print will not look exactly like the original. The working drawing is a guideline to composition, visual qualities, such as the relationship of line work and solid colour areas, and the overall scheme of colour. These elements have to be translated into the new medium and cannot be copied exactly, although in all media you can trace and transfer an image as your starting point – it is not necessary to redraw the composition from scratch.

For the inexperienced printmaker interested in producing prints in two or more colours, the working drawing is an essential step. You have to make a separate block, screen or plate for each main colour, and work out whether you can overprint colours to produce mixed hues. Sometimes, once you have isolated the areas for printing one colour, you will find that an originally realistic image is reduced to a series of more or less abstract shapes, and you cannot relate this to the other colours without some initial guideline. It may be best to make a fairly detailed working drawing and trace off each colour element with some accuracy. As you learn more of your craft, you can cut down the detail of this preliminary stage and simplify your plan to the bare essentials. Experienced printmakers may jump straight in without doing this at all because they feel confident of working direct with the print medium and can anticipate how the stages will gradually pull together.

Proofing and printing

In order to understand how the image is translating into print, proofs are taken at various stages. These working proofs also act as guidelines for further stages, such as the continued cutting of a block or processing of a plate; until you have seen the image as it prints you will not know where to develop it further or where to make corrections and adjustments.

From drawing to print
1 The composition of the still life is worked out in a detailed pencil and watercolour sketch to establish the overall shapes clearly and plot the colour and tonal variations within them. These are to be translated into a three-colour print – yellow, red, green – in which mixed hues will be achieved by overprinting.

2 Yellow is the dominant colour, contributing to each aspect of the still life, so it covers a broad area of the first printing plate. However, it will not have this full-strength effect in the final print. Being light-toned, it will recede somewhat against the other colours.

3 The red obviously has to be strongest in the tomatoes, and will print lightly over the yellow on the bowl in order to produce a warm orange. In the peppers, it is used tonally rather than as a distinct colour, to create the subtle shadows that model the forms.

4 The green printing has a more linear character, defining the contours of the forms quite strongly. As with the red, the colour has two functions, providing local colour in the green pepper and enhancing the detail and modelling of the red and yellow fruits.

On a relief block, you can take a rubbing rather than a printed proof, which is less laborious and gives you a fair idea of the image quality. An etching can be proofed at any stage, but on a mezzotint or drypoint plate the printing areas are relatively fragile – too many proofs cause the surface to deteriorate – so what you gain from proofing you may lose in the final printing.

When you are ready to take the final prints you can run a whole edition. An edition is a numbered set of identical prints – in commercial terms, the numbering is a safeguard of their value, and professional artists' plates or blocks are cancelled after an edition has been completed. The artist chooses the number of prints in an edition; sometimes it may depend on how the printing surface stands up to wear, as with drypoint and mezzotint. An artist's proof is a finished print that does not form part of the edition set – the first few trials of the final printing may become artist's proofs if the quality is good.

Inks and papers

The work done with the printmaking materials is not the only factor in the finished qualities of the print; the way you ink up the image and the paper you print on contribute other surface values. At the later stages of preparing any kind of print, your proof stages should ideally use the same inking procedure and type of

▲ **ELISABETH HARDEN**
PEPPERS AND TOMATOES (LITHOGRAPH)
The print is less heavily modelled than the original, since it contains no black that would correspond to the pencil drawing. The bright colours have a lush, fresh feeling appropriate to the subject. Dark shadows emerge from the overprinting of all three colours.

paper you intend for the finished version, as only then can you see the true effect.

Obviously different methods of printing require different properties from ink and paper, and proprietary-brand inks, available from specialist suppliers, are purpose-made for each one. Block-printing inks are more widely sold, and can be bought in most good art shops. In some cases – notably screenprinting and relief printing – you may find a choice between water-based or oil-based inks. Typically, oil-based types give the smoothest coverage and the most versatile effects, but the prints take longer to dry, and blocks or screens have to be cleaned up with the appropriate solvent. If in doubt, explain to the supplier what you intend to do and seek advice on the right type and texture of ink and colour ranges available to you. If you are studio-based, the supervising technician or tutor will advise.

Most relief and screenprints can be made on almost any kind of paper – even on fabric – but the weight, thickness and finish of the paper affects the appearance of the final image. Again, you may need to get advice on exactly what is needed in your case, but there are some basic guidelines you can follow.

For early proofing of block prints, screens and lithographs, inexpensive cartridge paper is quite adequate. Good-quality cartridge papers are also suitable for final proofs. Use a substantial kind, as thin papers may buckle under the ink.

For processes that involve dampening the paper, mainly the intaglio processes, do not use anything too flimsy or open-textured, such as unsized papers that may disintegrate when wetted. However, papers that are too thick and stiff will not penetrate the intaglio and will pick up a broken impression. The best papers for intaglio are good-quality drawing and watercolour papers, which come in a variety of weights, thicknesses and surface textures.

Avoid extremes of surface texture – on exceptionally smooth, coated papers, ink can slide or smudge easily. You might, for example, get a double impression if the paper slips on a relief block during printing. Equally, be wary of very thick, heavily toothed papers, which may resist the ink.

If you are interested in using decoratively coloured or textured papers, bear in mind that they will contribute specific qualities to the finished print which may not integrate appropriately. However, lightly toned, non-white papers – ivory or cream – and fibrous, lightweight Japanese papers are popular with printmakers. Strong base colours can be planned in as a specific element of an image; you can print white ink onto a coloured surface if required.

Papers
Different kinds of papers have practical purposes in printmaking, as well as providing the base material for the finished print. In intaglio printing, blotting and tissue papers (above, upper layers) are needed to prepare and store the dampened printing paper; prints can be taken on a variety of surfaces, including fine hand-made or good-quality mould-made drawing and watercolour papers (above). Textured and coloured papers (right) are useful for collage work and relief printing. To develop a printed image from an existing drawing or working study, you will also need tracing and transfer papers (below).

See also
Woodcuts; colour printing, pages 40–45

Monoprints

A monoprint, as its name implies, is a one-off impression made by applying printing ink to a flat surface and transferring it to paper. The method excludes one of the usual main purposes of printmaking, which is to obtain multiple copies of a single image, but the marks and textures obtained are characteristically different from those drawn or painted directly on paper. Monoprint is of particular interest to beginners in printmaking, because no presses or special studio equipment are needed.

Monoprint equipment
1 Brushes; **2** papers;
3 glass mixing slab;
4 block-printing inks;
5 palette knife; **6** roller.

Tools and materials
The printing surface can be anything which is flat, smooth and non-absorbent. Suitable materials are a sheet of glass, plastic or metal; a slab of polished stone; or a section of plastic-faced wood or composition board. To create your image, you can apply

Printing from glass
1 This method of preparing a monoprint image involves painting on the surface of the glass slab as you would on paper. The artist is using printing inks, and has placed a rough sketch underneath the glass as a guide.

2 The print is taken by laying paper on the glass and smoothing it down with your hand, a spoon or a roller. This produces a typically softer, more textured impression than the original painting.

block-printing inks (or oil paints) using any suitable implements – brushes, rollers, sticks, rags, sponges or palette knives – to build up the design, just as though you were drawing or painting on paper. Then you simply lay a sheet of paper over it and rub firmly but evenly across the back of the paper. When you lift the paper, the image is printed in reverse, as with relief-printing methods.

Developing the print
Monoprints can be graphic monochrome studies or vigorous multi-coloured images. You can also overprint; for example, to build up thin colour 'glazes', develop dark tones or lay in line work over solid colour areas. You do this by taking your first print, then cleaning off the working surface and reworking with ink to take a second impression.

To overprint accurately, you need to use a simple form of registration. You can simply align the paper to the edges of the surface you are printing from, or if this is not large enough to give a good margin of paper around the printed image, you can lay a larger registration sheet beneath, visible on at least two sides, and align the printing paper to that. In the demonstration sequence shown here, the artist places a working sketch beneath the sheet of glass as a guide for each painting stage and for registration of overprintings.

Although you cannot produce a series of prints by re-inking, as you can with an etched plate or incised block, you can sometimes obtain two or three impressions from one inking; they will gradually become fainter, coarser textured and less colourful. There are various ways you can experiment with this medium, apart from the way you prepare the initial design. Variations in the thickness of the ink and the pressure you apply to the paper will affect both the tone and texture of the print.

2 By dragging and lifting the ink with a rag dampened with white spirit, she draws free, broad shapes in the colour area.

3 The paper is placed over the glass sheet, aligned to the left-hand edge of the working drawing below the glass, and the print is taken by hand-rubbing. This gives a soft, moody monochrome image.

Printing from acetate
If you work on acetate sheet rather than glass, you can take the print on a press rather than by hand. The additional pressure makes the colours stronger and the textures more detailed.

Overprinting
1 For the first stage of a three-stage print, the artist rolls out a flat layer of thin ink on glass. A sketch guide is positioned underneath the glass.

4 The second stage is prepared by painting on the glass with several colours. The underlying sketch is the guide for positioning the colours so they will overprint accurately on the monochrome image.

5 The monochrome print is aligned to the left-hand edge of the paper beneath the glass and laid down over the painting, which is again printed off by hand-rubbing on the back of the paper.

6 The artist partially removes the painting by cleaning it off with white spirit on a rag. She then reworks the dark-toned areas with fresh ink and takes a third impression.

7 In the finished print, the overprinting has produced a variety of tones and textures that create a simply stated but highly atmospheric image.

Linear drawing

1 Block-printing ink is rolled out thinly on the glass slab. The colour areas are roughly estimated in relation to the subject to be drawn.

2 A sheet of paper is laid down over the ink, and the wooden end of a paintbrush is used to draw on the back of the paper. Alternatively, you can use a pencil, knitting needle or other suitable implement.

Developing textures

1 This experimental sequence investigates patterns and textures relating to water and wave patterns. Coloured inks are squeezed onto the glass directly from the tube.

3 The impression shows a soft but strong line quality that gives an expressive character to the drawing. The background is lightly textured through contact with the rolled-out colours.

2 A simple blotting off onto paper spreads the ink marks and produces a vigorously textured surface. There is always a random element to these very basic printing techniques.

3 The artist works into the painting on glass by blotting the colours again and adding fresh ink. The top band of the colour layers is rolled out to create a feeling of the division between sea and sky.

4 Paper is placed over the ink, and using a pencil the artist begins to draw roughly scribbled wave patterns, working the hatched textures in different directions.

5 Progress can be checked at any stage by peeling back the paper; keep one edge in place so that the paper goes back in exactly the same position. If the image is not strong enough, the pressure of the pencil marks can be varied or reworked.

6 This impression has a looser, busier texture than the simple blotted-off image in Step 2. The movements of the pencil create a more active surface in the finished print.

Linocut

■ PLANNING THE IMAGE

■ CUTTING THE BLOCK

■ PROOFING AND PRINTING

■ COLOUR PRINTING

This is an excellent printmaking technique for the complete beginner. The process of preparing the block is relatively simple, and after only a little experiment with the tools you can quickly produce a strikingly original image, either monochrome or multi-coloured. A printing press is not essential, so you can satisfactorily complete the process without access to specialised studio facilities.

Lino is a sympathetic medium in that it is relatively soft and easy to cut, but because of its pliability, it is not suitable for very fine line work, which can break down in the course of cutting or printing. Monochrome linocuts make use of the material's strong graphic potential, exploiting bold shapes and patterns. Printing in two or three colours allows many possibilities for texturing and shading the image.

Tools and materials

Lino is a corky, composite sheet material with a hessian backing. You can obtain small pre-cut lino blocks from most art-material shops, and large pieces or rolls up to 1 metre (3ft) wide from specialist suppliers of printmaking materials.

The quality of lino varies; sometimes the block is very smooth and compact, but the texture can also be grainy and liable to crumble when cut. It deteriorates with age, becoming hard and brittle. Warming the block before you start cutting helps to soften a 'difficult' texture, easing the passage of the tools. Lino has a naturally oily feel, but the surface can be de-greased before you start work by wiping with methylated spirits or rubbing gently with a fine-grade sandpaper.

The principal linocutting tools are gouges and V-tools of different sizes. You can also use an ordinary craft knife to cut grooves in the block or to outline areas to be cleared with the gouges. Blunt tools can easily tear the soft lino, so they should be kept sharp.

The block is inked with a roller. Different sizes and types are available, made of rubber, gelatin or plastic. Inexpensive rollers are often too hard to give even coverage; a softer roller is more sensitive to any variations in the lino surface.

Linocut equipment
1, 2 Palette knife and push knife, for mixing inks; **3** tap knife for cutting lino; **4** spoon for hand-printing; **5** roller; **6** lino; **7** gouges; **8** V-tools; **9** baren, a purpose-made tool for hand-printing.

Sharpening a gouge
1 Place the curved blade of the gouge on an oilstone and rock it from side to side so the whole edge makes contact with the stone.

2 Sharpen the inner edge of the blade with a broad slipstone. Support the tool firmly while rubbing the stone back and forth.

Sharpening a V-tool
1 Put one side of the blade flat on the oilstone and rub it back and forth. Repeat with the other side to sharpen both outer facets and the point between them.

2 To sharpen the inner edges, you need a fine slipstone that fits into the 'V'. Support the shaft of the tool as for the gouge, while moving the stone inside the blade.

Planning the image

You can mark out your design in pencil, marker or Indian ink applied with brush or pen, de-greasing the surface first if necessary. If you are using a working drawing, you can trace this down on the block using transfer paper. Remember, however, that the image will appear reversed when printed; if you want it to read the same way round as the original, reverse the tracing before you transfer it to the block.

Alternatively, you can make the original drawing directly on the block, as shown here. If you make errors, you can either draw over them, remembering to ignore the incorrect lines when you begin to cut, or you can wipe out the error with a suitable solvent and rework the area completely.

Shapes in a linocut design can be cut positively or negatively: that is, you can cut around the outline of the shape or you can remove the whole area within the outline. When working in monochrome, you need to plan the interaction of lines and shapes carefully, working out what to do with the edges where two or more shapes butt together, and how to vary and contrast areas of plain colour and pattern.

1

2

3

4

Gouge marks
1 The gouge makes a bold stroke that can be clean-edged or lightly toothed. This sample shows long and short cuts with (from left to right) medium-sized, fine and broad gouges. The rough-edged mark is made by easing the tool from side to side, as well as forwards through the lino.

V-tool marks
2 This sample shows a comparable range of marks made with medium-sized, fine and broad V-tools. The beginning of the cut is slightly tapered where the 'V' bites into the lino. You can end the cut with a taper by easing the tool up gradually, or you can form a squared end by stopping the stroke abruptly.

Developing texture
3 A more complex textured effect can be obtained by quite simple means when you are overprinting colours. This shows where the same marks of the V-tool have been re-cut more broadly for the black printing.

Line and tone
4 The tools can be used to cut the main shape in outline or to cut away the surrounding areas, leaving the outline in relief. You may even wish to combine the two approaches in one design and should plan how you will make the transition between solid shapes and line work.

Drawing on the block
1 For this demonstration of cutting a monochrome image, the artist works directly from the subject, drawing on the block with a black waxy pencil.

3 The pattern on the plate is indicated very loosely, leaving the artist an open choice as to how to treat those areas as the cutting of the design develops.

2 The markings on the fish form the most intricate part of the design and they are drawn in some detail. The shape of the plate has been drawn to position the whole design on the centre of the block.

Cutting the block

There is no particular order or sequence to cutting into the design. For example, you can begin with narrow cuts outlining the overall shapes, then work into detail and clear any large 'white' areas; or you can work from one side to another, completing each section as you go. You will soon learn to judge which tools provide the right width of cut and how much pressure you need to apply. Avoid working too heavily, as it is easy to slip and cut into a section that should be left uncut. Move the tool easily and evenly; if you angle a knife or V-tool blade too sharply, you may undercut the lino, which makes lines and edges unstable.

If you have a large area to clear which is 'non-reading' in the print, or you are shaping the outer edges of the block, you need not do all the work with the gouges. You can cut away the surplus lino with a craft knife or scissors.

Cutting the block
1 Initially, a V-tool is used to establish fine outlines and work into the detail of each fish head and body.

2 Once the markings of both fishes have been described with careful line work, the artist begins to clear the white areas, working rapidly with a broad gouge.

3 The gouge is used roughly so the lowered surface of the block retains some relief texture that will print.

4 The outer border around the design is not to print at all. Rather than clear it with a gouge, the artist cuts the lino away. The shape of the plate is outlined with a V-tool, then cuts are made from the edge towards the outline.

Proofing and printing

For a monochrome print like the example shown here, you can check the progress of the cutting without actually rolling up and printing the block. Simply place a piece of paper over the surface and take a rubbing with a pencil. This will be accurate enough to show you where further cutting is required, and whether there is a good balance of negative and positive areas.

When the block is ready to print, roll out the ink thinly on the inking slab, then roll it over the raised areas of the lino firmly and evenly. You can work back and forth in all directions, and if you put down too much ink you can take up some of the excess by running the roller in one direction only.

You can take a print either by placing paper over the block and rubbing with a baren, a spoon or any other smooth, curved tool; or you can print on a flat-bed, cylinder or proofing press.

Proofing and printing
1 Rather than ink the block to pull a proof, the artist takes a rubbing on thin paper with a graphite pencil. Any refinements needed can be cleanly cut before printing.

5 The edge-cuts make the lino more flexible, allowing the scissors to ease accurately around the circular shape. If the border area were cut with a gouge, some residual marks might appear on the print, but removing the surplus ensures a clean outline.

4 Position the inked block on a clean sheet of paper on the bed of the press. Align the printing paper to the base sheet, so the printed image will be centrally placed, and lower the paper onto the block.

2 When the design is complete, it can be inked and printed. To roll ink out evenly, spread it across the glass slab with a palette knife, then work outwards with the roller until the ink forms a thin coating.

5 Activate the press to exert even pressure on the block and paper. Take hold of one corner of the printing paper and peel it back gently from the block.

3 You can work in all directions when rolling up the block. Go over it as many times as you need to coat it evenly with colour, picking up more ink on the roller as necessary.

Printing without a press

1 If you have no access to a press, you can use this hand-printing method, also known as burnishing. Ink the block and position it on a clean base sheet. Lay the printing paper over it.

2 Use a rounded implement such as a purpose-made baren, the back of a spoon or, as here, an etching dabber wrapped in muslin, to rub firmly and evenly all over the back of the printing sheet.

3 A print taken by this method is lighter coloured than one taken on a press, because the pressure is less intense. As you continue to take prints and the ink layer on the block builds up, the image becomes darker and more even.

6 The completed print has a bold, graphic style, with crisp black line work nicely offset by the incidental patches of rough texture in the whites. Variations in the line widths give a pleasing 'hand-done' quality without detracting from the clarity of the image.

Colour printing

Multi-coloured linocuts can be prepared by one of two methods. In the reduction process, successive cuts are made in the same block, and a new colour is printed at various stages. The other method is to register the design on separate blocks, one for each colour. The reduction method (see pages 40–45) may be easier to register for printing, as it is the same block you are using at each stage; but the block is gradually destroyed by the continuing work, so you have to be confident about how much of the surface is to be removed for each printing.

Using two or more blocks gives you more time to think through the cutting stages, and you can proof all the colours to compare and amend the different areas. However, any slight variations in the dimensions or shape of the blocks' outer edges can make it difficult to align each printing.

To cut two or more blocks, you can use a master tracing to place the image on each, but a more accurate method is to cut the first block and use it as the key block for offsetting the image onto the uncut lino pieces. As shown here, the method used to register block and paper for the offsetting is then also used to register the overprintings.

Offsetting and overprinting
1 Cut your block for the first colour, using the appropriate marks and textures for the effect that you wish to achieve.

2 Ink up the first block in black and lay it centred on a clean sheet of paper on the bed of the press. With a pencil, mark the edges and corners of the block on the base sheet. This sheet will form your guide for registering subsequent printings. Take a print from the block on smooth paper.

3 Lay the uncut second block in the marked area on the base sheet and place the black print over it, aligned to the edges of the base sheet. Run this through the press so that the print transfers colour onto the clean lino block.

Registering on the press
This method of registration is a simple alternative to the use of a base sheet, as shown in the main sequence. Mark the positions for the block and printing paper directly on the bed of the press, using small strips of card attached with masking tape. Butt the corner of the block to the inner cards. Next slip the corner of the paper in to align with the outer registration stops before lowering the full sheet over the block.

4 Use the shapes offset from the first block as a guide to cutting your design for the second colour. Pay special attention to areas where the two colours will overprint, and any shapes that must register exactly.

5 Roll up and print the first block in the required colour. Here it is printed in red: this is the same block that was printed black in Steps 2 and 3 to offset the image.

6 You may find it helpful to mark one corner of the base sheet and the corresponding corner of the print with a small cross: each time you come to print, from a second or subsequent block, match the crosses and then align from that corner. This is particularly valuable when you are printing several colours, as the prints can appear quite abstract in the early stages and it is easy to make an error in overprinting.

7 Roll up the second block in the required colour – in this example it is to print black over red. Position the block on the base sheet, register the printed image over it and run them through the press.

8 This extremely lively image combines solid blocks of colour with roughly worked gouged textures and bold patterns made with the V-tool. The registration of colours on the figure is deliberately inexact to add to the sense of movement, but, where required, background shapes have overprinted cleanly along the same outlines.

See also
Woodcuts:
colour printing,
pages 40–45

Woodcut

- CUTTING THE BLOCK

- COLOUR PRINTING

Woodcut printing is very similar in technique and process to linocut, but different in style and surface quality due to the properties of the base material. Woodcuts are made on the side grain of the wood, and the natural pattern and direction of the grain are integrated with the textures and patterns made by the cutting process.

In linocutting, the tools cut easily in all directions, but for woodcuts it is easier to cut along or with the grain than across or against it. The type of wood used – how heavily grained and hard or soft it is – will also affect the print. You can obtain interesting variations between clean and ragged edges, sharp knife cuts or broadly gouged channels. Woodcuts are associated with the aggressive, jagged graphics of European Expressionists, but also with the clarity and formality of Japanese colour prints, so a wide range of variations is possible.

Tools and materials

A useful aspect of the woodcut process for beginners is that you can use almost any type of wood. Instead of buying specially prepared blocks, you can pick up offcuts of plyboard or timber from a woodyard. Pine boards and plywood sheets, inexpensive and readily available, are highly suitable for trying out the cutting techniques and gaining confidence with the medium. They are relatively coarse and liable to splinter, but are also soft to cut and have pleasing, pronounced grain patterns. As you become interested in the process of woodcut and practised in the techniques, you can investigate finer, denser woods that allow more delicate control. The only way to discover and exploit the characteristics of different types is to try them.

Tools for woodcut include the V-tools and gouges also used for linocut. The interchangeable gouge sets, however, are unsuitable because they are not strong enough; use the metal-shafted individual gouges. Cutting knives are extensively used in woodcut; specialist tools are available from printmaking suppliers, or you can use a sturdy craft knife. Chisels are also useful tools for abrading the surface and clearing large areas.

Prints are made from wood blocks in exactly the same way as from lino: the surface is inked and the print can be taken by hand or on a press. Thin plyboard can be printed on a cylinder or flat-bed press. A thick wood block must be printed by the direct pressure of a flat-bed press, or on a type-proofing press where the block can be packed into a sunken bed and the paper rolled over it.

2

Woodcut equipment
1 Side-grain wood blocks;
2 gouges and V-tools; **3** craft
knife; **4** cutting knife for fine line
work on block; **5, 6** push knife and
palette knife; **7** block-printing ink.

Cutting the block

Some artists cut directly into the block without preparation. Others may prepare the surface by sandpapering or brushing with a wire brush to remove any loose fibres and bring up the grain pattern. As with lino, you can draw onto the surface with pencils, markers or brush and ink, or trace down a design using transfer paper. You can, if you wish, stain the surface all over by rubbing it with diluted printing ink; this enables you to see the cut marks very clearly as you progress.

Wood is quite a responsive surface, and you can obtain good effects from a variety of different marks. Try to get the feel of the tool as you cut, particularly as you change its angle to the grain. Pushing a gouge easily along the grain produces even, clean-edged cuts, but cutting too boldly across it can cause major splintering that strips too much of the surface.

The width of the gouge you choose has to be matched to the elements of your design, but otherwise the choice of tool is a matter of common sense – there is obviously more labour involved in trying to clear a large area with a narrow gouge than with a wide one. In an open area, you may leave small ridges that will print as a broken texture; this can be effective, but if, after proofing, you find it is not suitable, you can clean up the shape and remove any cutting marks.

Cutting the block
1 Unless your design is small-scale, or you are very confident in cutting, it is best to draw a fairly detailed outline of the image on the wood block.

Using gouges and V-tools
1 All woodcut tools cut most easily along the grain of the wood. A small gouge makes clean-edged fine lines suitable for outlining or hatched textures.

2 The print shows how the grain of the wood contributes a specific background texture, where the relief surface is allowed to print as large areas of dark tone.

3 Broad gouges are used for line work. In addition, by keeping the cuts close together or overlapping them, broad gouges can be used to clear areas of the block.

4 Pushing the gouge across rather than along the grain, you encounter more resistance and may need to ease the gouge from side to side as it moves forwards.

2 In this example, the image depends upon some intricate pattern-making in the structures of the buildings. The artist draws this in detail, filling in lines and shapes that feature strongly.

3 The artist begins cutting the broadest lines, stripping the wood rapidly with a gouge. As with lino, there is no particular rule as to where you should start.

4 Because the print will consist of a four-colour sequence, the cutting at this stage is relatively limited, consisting only of those elements that will appear white in the final print. Fine detail is worked with a narrow gouge.

5 Although the width of the tool mark does not vary much, you can see how working along or across the grain produces different edge qualities.

6 The V-tool reacts similarly to the gouge in terms of the direction it takes. However, if the angled blade is sharp, the cross-grain resistance may be less influential because the cutting edge is less broad.

7 A V-tool cut begins sharply and broadens as the full width of the blade bites into the wood. Short, angular cuts produce interesting coarse textures.

8 The actual character of each mark may be less important than the way the tools are used to cut particular elements in the design, but this sample block demonstrates a wide range of textures obtained with only three tools.

Colour printing

This demonstration shows a four-colour wood block cut and printed by the reduction method. In the first cutting, only the areas to remain white are taken out, and the block is printed with the first colour rolled all over the surface. In the second stage, the areas to remain as the first colour – in this case a light-toned beige – are removed, and the whole block is printed in yellow. In the third stage, the areas to remain yellow are cut out and the block is printed in blue. Finally, the blue areas are cut away and the remaining relief surface is overprinted in black ink.

With the reduction method it is not necessary to follow the process of offsetting demonstrated for linocut, but you can use the same registration process to ensure that the colours overprint accurately. In this case, however, having printed the first colour, the artist registers the block for each subsequent printing by laying it face down on the print rather than aligning the paper over the block. For this you need a confident eye and steady hands.

Printing and overprinting
1 When the first stage of cutting is complete, you can immediately print the first colour (you may wish to take one proof first to check the balance of the image and the effectiveness of individual shapes). Roll up the whole block with an even layer of ink.

2 Run the print through the press and peel back the paper carefully. Once you have begun to lift the paper, it is advisable not to lay it back down, as any slight shift can create a double image.

3 At the second cutting stage, remove all areas of the block that will appear as the first colour – in this case, beige – in the final print.

4 If you have to mix a special colour when printing, make sure you have a quantity that will cover the number of prints you wish to make; it can be difficult to match a mixed hue.

5 Roll up the block in the second colour, working in all directions to produce an even coating of ink. It is advisable to have a roller that relates well to the size of the block. A large brayer is being used here.

6 To register the second colour over the first, the artist lays the block face down on the original print, judging the alignment of edges and corners by eye.

7 The cutting in the third stage consists of removing all the areas of the image that should appear yellow in the final print. An experienced artist may work directly on the block; for a beginner, it is helpful to use a previously prepared colour study as a guide.

8 There may be a lot of detailed cutting at the final stage, because in order to allow the previous three colours to show through, much of the remaining relief surface becomes linear in character.

9 Large areas of the block have now been cleared, particularly the sky, which is very open. The cutting is deliberately rough, so that a lightly textured impression will show up between the more emphatic lines.

Stage proof: one

In a print made by the reduction method, the first colour printing may include a lot of broad, flat colour areas where the detail will be created by the cutting for subsequent colours. When printing is completed, clean the ink from the block immediately with solvent and a rag.

Stage proof: two

The second colour printing begins to suggest the three-dimensional depth in the image, but because the two colours are close in tone, the change is not dramatic.

Stage proof: three
The overprinting in blue, using the same registration technique as for the yellow, produces a more appreciable variation in the image, both because the colour is lighter than those underneath and because the textures are becoming more complex.

Stage proof: four
The black printing sharpens the image and gives it a much bolder, more graphic feeling, pulling together all the shapes. This is the effect that the artist has been carrying in her mind throughout the cutting processes. The radical changes that occur with each successive stage are a very exciting feature of colour printing. Although with experience you can anticipate many aspects of the colour interactions, the overall result can still contain surprising and unexpectedly pleasing details.

Wood engraving

- CUTTING THE BLOCK
- PROOFING AND PRINTING

Wood engraving is a much finer, more delicate process than woodcut. The cutting is done on the end-grain of the wood, which has a very tight texture. The grain is not a feature of the design – the image is created entirely by the cut marks.

The techniques of wood engraving are precise and controlled, but you can achieve a wide variety of marks and textures. For practical reasons wood engravings are usually small-scale, and it is easier to produce an image that reads as white lines on black than to clear areas of the block leaving black lines in relief. It is typically a monochrome method (although the relief surface can be inked in any colour) since the engraved work is too detailed and tight to allow re-cutting and overprinting that can be exploited with side-grain wood and lino. Printing in black, or a very dark-toned colour, best conveys the subtle graphic effects of the engraving.

Tools and materials

The preferred wood for end-grain blocks is box, which has a tight grain but is relatively soft and easy to engrave. This is a slow-growing, small tree, so wood-engraving blocks are usually only 5–8cm (2–3in) across – larger blocks are made by jointing small pieces together. The wood must be properly seasoned and prepared, so blocks should be bought from a specialist supplier, which can be expensive. Holly, pear or maple are cheaper substitutes that may also be available. Compact blocks of manufactured board or plywood can also be used.

The engraving tools are fine shafts of metal, faceted and sharpened to form various shapes of cutting tip. The main types are the lozenge-shaped graver for general line work; the elliptical spitsticker, designed for cutting curves; the squared or rounded scorper, used for broad marks and clearing areas of the block; and the fine tint tool, which maintains a line of uniform width. It is important to keep the tools sharp, as blunt tools slip and slide on the close-grained surface.

To cut curves and angles, you turn the block rather than the tool. To facilitate the movement it can be mounted on the traditional engraver's sandbag, but you can work just as effectively by resting the block on a book wrapped in a cloth. Raising the block also helps you to grip it and hold it steady.

The block-printing ink for wood engraving should be quite stiff, otherwise it may flood the delicate marks. A small gelatin or rubber roller is adequate for inking the little wood blocks. Prints can be taken easily by hand, using a spoon or baren to rub the back of the paper.

1

Wood-engraving equipment
1 End-grain wood blocks;
2 engraving tools; **3** glass mixing
slab; **4** block-printing ink; **5** palette
knife; **6** roller.

Holding the tools
1 Fit the mushroom-shaped wooden handle of the tool into your palm and support the metal shaft lightly with your fingers. Grip the shaft close to the cutting tip with forefinger and thumb.

2 For engraving straight lines and curves, keep the tool at a shallow angle to the working surface, allowing the pressure of your whole hand to move it forwards.

3 For short cuts, such as fine and coarse stippling, raise the tool at a sharper angle so that the action of the cutting tip is naturally abbreviated.

Marks of the tools

This test block and print show some of the variations of texture that can be achieved with different tools handled in different ways. On the print, these are: (top, left to right) stippling with a coarse graver; dashes cut with a spitsticker; close stippling with a fine graver; (bottom, left to right) short cuts with a scorper; lines cut with a scorper; lines cut with a spitsticker.

Sharpening tools

1 To sharpen a graver, put the facet of the cutting tip flat down on the oilstone and rub with a circular motion.

2 To sharpen a scarper, put the underside of the cutting tip on the oilstone and move it back and forth. Repeat with both flat sides of the narrow blade.

Cutting the block

A drawing can be made directly on the block or a prepared design can be traced down. If you are working in a way that produces a white-line image, you may find it easiest to darken the surface of the block with ink. You can then make your tracing with white transfer paper, so that the initial drawing will correspond to what you expect to see in the print.

For line work, the tool is held at a shallow angle to the block; the shape is designed for this, with the shaft broadly angled away from the wooden handle. The cutting needs to be quite slow and precise: because you are working on a small area, a too-forceful stroke can cause a significant error.

Drawing on the block
1 Paint the upper surface of the block with a thin coat of black drawing ink and allow it to dry completely.

2 Place a piece of white, or light-coloured, transfer paper on the block and put your drawing over it. Tape the papers to the edge of the block and go over the design in pencil to trace it down.

3 The transferred drawing in white on black gives an idea of the way the print will appear, but you do not need to fill in all the detail at this stage – this can be developed as you cut.

Cutting the block
1 Support the block on a raised surface while you cut, so you can hold it firmly by its edges. A book wrapped in cloth is the support used here.

2 Work into different areas of the design with the appropriate tool. This picture shows a graver being used for stippled detail.

3 The scorper is used to draw strong lines and to clear small areas of the block; note the shallow angle of the tip on the surface.

4 Work the cutting to a more or less finished stage before taking a proof. Most of the detail should be in place, with only minor refinements to do after proofing.

Proofing and printing

Once you have inked the block to take a proof it is less easy to see the design clearly, as the ink will have stained some of the finer lines. Proofing is therefore best left until the work is quite advanced. You can then make any refinements needed in the cutting before you take final prints. Do not clean off the ink with a solvent after proofing – just wipe it with a rag to remove the excess.

In keeping with the overall character of the process, the method of inking should be careful and controlled. You need only make one pass of the roller over the block in each direction. It is important not to over-ink the relief surface or the colour will spread into and fill the engraved lines.

Proofing and printing
1 Roll out the ink on a glass mixing slab. Use quite a stiff block-printing ink so it will not flood the delicate lines cut into the wood block.

2 Roll up the surface of the block, being careful not to over-ink. You need only make one pass of the roller in each direction across the surface.

3 Use a lightweight printing paper that will pick up all the detail. Because the block is small, it is easy to take the proof by burnishing with the back of a spoon. Place the paper on the block and rub it down firmly.

4 When you see the result of the proof, you can decide what further work is necessary before final prints are taken. Here, the artist decides some extra highlighting is needed.

5 Before continuing to cut, wipe the excess ink off the block with a clean rag. Do not use a solvent, as this will flood the cuts and stain them, making it difficult to see the design.

6 As the final stage on this engraving, the artist uses a graver to cut a halo of fine stippling around the butterfly shape (below).

7 This attractive image demonstrates the small-scale character of wood engraving and the way it is necessary to balance the tones and textures by controlling the weight and direction of the various marks.

Collage blocks

This area of printmaking provides the opportunity to produce interesting and varied printed images without the use of specialist materials and tools.

The basic principle of relief printing, in which the design is formed by the contrast between positive (raised) areas of the printing block and negative (cut-away) sections, can be adapted to hand-made blocks constructed from a wide range of materials. These are assembled on a flat base to form a relief block with different surface levels. Suitable materials include paper, cardboard, fabric and string; found objects such as bottle tops and buttons; or acrylic mediums, which are applied in fluid form but dry to form hard, rubbery textures.

The technique has the same relationship to linocut or woodcut as collage has to painting. Instead of manipulating one material to create your effects, you combine different substances and textures. You ink with a roller as if it were a wood or lino block. To print, you can use the hand-burnishing method of rubbing the paper down onto the inked block with a spoon or similar tool, although using a relief-printing press gives you a stronger, denser image (see pages 31–33).
The term collagraph refers to a collaged block printed in the same way as an intaglio plate

9

1

2

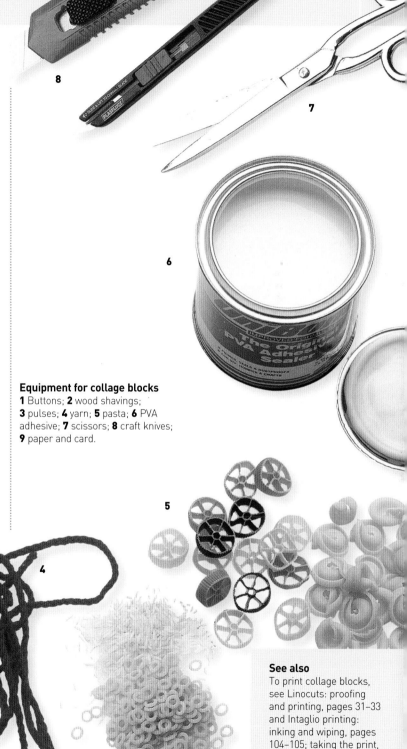

(see pages 106–107). To print the block effectively it must be run through an intaglio printing press, so the collage should not be too thick – about 8mm (¼in) – so it will pass between the rollers easily.

Tools and materials

The only tools you need are a craft knife and scissors for cutting your materials and a roller for inking up the block. Choosing materials for the collage is a matter of judgement and experience. It is not possible to predict absolutely the effect a particular material will make. Sometimes the roller picks up much more or less of the surface texture than you anticipate, though you can adjust the effects a little in the pressures you apply to inking up and printing. It is useful to experiment with small samples before selecting materials for a particular kind of image.

Among the simplest and most readily available materials are different kinds of card and papers – you can save offcuts and packaging materials, looking out for varied weights and textures. String, wool, ribbon and braid are all effective. Adhesive tapes are useful for forming linear and geometric motifs.

An all-purpose acrylic adhesive such as PVA or Marvin medium works as both the means of glueing materials to the support and as an independent printing element. The viscous white medium can be thickly applied with a pen, brush or knife; it dries into a clear, rubbery surface that retains its original texture and prints well. It also makes an excellent binder for loose, textured materials such as sand or rice.

The number of impressions you can take depends upon the resilience of the materials you have used – the surface will eventually break down, especially if some of the materials are absorbent. Sealing the surface with a thin application of acrylic medium makes the collage more durable.

Equipment for collage blocks
1 Buttons; **2** wood shavings; **3** pulses; **4** yarn; **5** pasta; **6** PVA adhesive; **7** scissors; **8** craft knives; **9** paper and card.

See also
To print collage blocks, see Linocuts: proofing and printing, pages 31–33 and Intaglio printing: inking and wiping, pages 104–105; taking the print, pages 106–107.

Braid and yarn
Scraps of fancy braids and yarns from a knitting or sewing basket contribute unusual pattern qualities. Because the materials are absorbent, you may need to ink and print a few times before the full impression comes through.

Cardboard
In addition to selecting different textures and thicknesses of cardboard to create variations in your print, you can cut into the surface and peel back the top layer to make hard edges and rough, broken textures.

Sandpaper
The gritty surface of sandpaper prints a fine pattern of irregular dots. The solid colour at the top edge of this section comes from tearing the material so that the abrasive layer is pulled away, leaving only the base paper.

String

Pieces of string create distinct, fine lines, but with a pleasing burred texture. Different effects will be obtained according to the weight and thickness of the string and the fibres from which it is made.

Adhesive tapes

Masking tape has a rough finish that prints as a mottled or striated texture. Smooth, finer tapes allow the ink to print off more evenly. The edges print as dark or light lines, depending on the thickness of the tape.

Split peas

Loose materials such as pulses, sand or wood chippings can be glued to the collage base by pressing them into a layer of acrylic medium and allowing it to dry. The patterns that print are more random than you might expect, in this case because the hard peas have irregular surfaces.

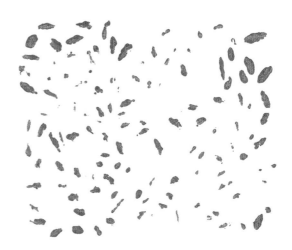

Rice

A hand-proofed print from a layer of rice stuck in acrylic medium produces a coarse stipple effect. With all such materials you will obtain a slightly stronger texture if you print on a press, because of the more intense, even contact between printing surface and paper.

Glue painting

1 A thick acrylic adhesive can be painted onto cardboard in rough shapes and drawn into with the wooden end of the paintbrush, or with a pencil. The medium is opaque white while wet, so you can see what you are doing, but dries clear.

Making the collage

1 The materials are glued to a cardboard base; let the adhesive dry completely before printing. This example is a hilly landscape constructed from various thicknesses and finishes of cardboard, sandpaper and string, and crumpled tissue for the sky.

2 Because the medium is applied in liquid form, the surface areas are slightly curved, which becomes more apparent as the glue painting dries. In this case only the highest ridges have printed, giving the effect of a free, bold line drawing.

2 In the first proof the softer cardboard layers reveal a 'honeycomb' texture under the pressure of printing. This appears too evenly distributed and mechanical, so additional materials are added to the block.

3 This proof has a more satisfactory contrast of textured and solid colour areas. In the foreground, thin card pieces create strong black shapes; the upper slopes of the hills are more densely textured where a thick layer of acrylic medium has been loosely brushed on.

Screenprinting

■ HAND-CUT STENCILS

■ PAPER STENCILS

■ FILLER STENCILS

■ TUSCHE METHOD

The principle of screenprinting differs from that of the other printmaking processes in that the print is taken not by the direct impression of one surface upon another, but by printing through an intermediary surface – the screen mesh. The images of screenprints are formed by various kinds of stencilling techniques, based on blocking out areas of the mesh either with sheet materials, such as paper or stencil film, or with liquids that fill the mesh.

As well as being a fine-art process, screenprinting has a direct association with commercial and industrial printing processes, being used extensively in graphic, ceramic and textile design. It is a colourful, versatile medium which you can adapt to the context of your work.

Tools and materials

The basic equipment consists of the screen – a wooden frame that has a fine-mesh fabric stretched over it – and the squeegee. This is a rubber blade set in a handle, with which the screen ink is pulled across the mesh. The mesh transmits an even coating of ink which adheres to the paper below the screen.

The stencil, whatever its form, seals certain areas of the screen so that the ink cannot pass through, thus creating positive and negative colour areas. The stencil can be a material as simple as thin paper that will adhere to the underside of the mesh – for example, newsprint, tracing paper or greaseproof paper. Stencil film is a gelatinous material on a plastic backing that can be cut with a sharp craft knife – when soaked with water it softens and is pressed into the mesh before the backing is removed. A similar effect can be obtained with self-adhesive plastic film applied to the screen, and you can also use adhesive tapes. Paper and film stencils produce clean-cut, hard-edged images.

Materials that are pre-cut and then applied to the screen are known as indirect stencils, while those which are applied by painting and drawing are called direct stencils. 'Liquid stencils', or screen fillers, may be water-soluble, oil-based or cellulose. The type you use depends on the type of ink, as the filler must remain resistant to the solvent of the ink so that the stencil remains intact when you print

2

6

and clean the ink from the screen. Commonly, water-based fillers are used in combination with oil-based inks. Conversely, you can combine oil-based filler with water-based inks. Cellulose filler is impervious to both oil- and water-based inks, but has to be cleaned from the mesh with a special solvent.

Screenprinting equipment
1 Squeegee; **2** screen;
3 screenprinting inks; **4** palette knife; **5** solvent brush to remove stencils; **6** cleaning rags.

See also
Screenprinting: filler stencils, pages 70–73

Hand-cut stencils

The advantage of using hand-cut stencils is that all the elements of the printed image are prepared away from the screen. If you get something completely wrong, you can remake the stencil. When cutting film stencils, you can see through the material, so it can be placed over a working drawing to guide the cutting.

When you plan the image you must take into account that paper or film stencils give you hard-edged, graphic shapes. Each colour to be printed requires a separate stencil. If the ink is fairly transparent, you can obtain colour 'mixtures' by overprinting one hue on another, and build up quite complex effects of pattern and form by varying the shapes and details of each overprinting. The process of registering colour printings on the screen bed is quite simple.

Where colour areas are to be butted together you should allow a very tiny overlap when cutting the separate stencils for each colour, as otherwise you may get a white line between them as you print the colours individually. The demonstration sequence shows both the processes of preparing hand-cut stencils and the basic methods of inking and printing. The simple technique of laying out ink and pulling the squeegee across the mesh is standard however the screen stencils are prepared.

Preparing hand-cut stencils
1 Stencil film has two layers – the coloured stencil and a clear backing sheet. Use a fine scalpel to cut lightly into the top layer. Here the artist is using a working sketch slipped under the stencil as a guide.

2 When you have cut a shape in outline, use the point of the knife to lift one edge or corner, then peel back the cut shape.

3 Prepare stencils for each of the colours you are to print and check that the shapes align by overlaying them one on another. In this demonstration, six colours are to be printed: pink, yellow, light blue, red, mid-blue and black.

4 Position the stencil under the screen mesh. Because a large screen is being used here, and the stencils are relatively small, the artist is placing three stencils side by side on one screen.

5 Lower the screen so the mesh lies flat on the stencil and spray clean water on the mesh. This softens the stencil material so it will adhere to the screen. You must move on quickly to the next stage.

6 Lay a clean piece of newsprint over the screen and blot firmly with your hands, creating pressure that sticks the stencil to the mesh. Because this has to be done quickly, if you are putting more than one stencil on the screen, do each in turn rather than all together.

7 When all of the stencils adhere to the screen, allow them to dry out completely. You can speed up the process by using a hot-air dryer.

8 To block out the open areas of the screen mesh surrounding the stencils, turn the screen upside down and spread a liquid filler around the borders. The simplest way to do this is to use a small piece of card to pull the liquid across the mesh.

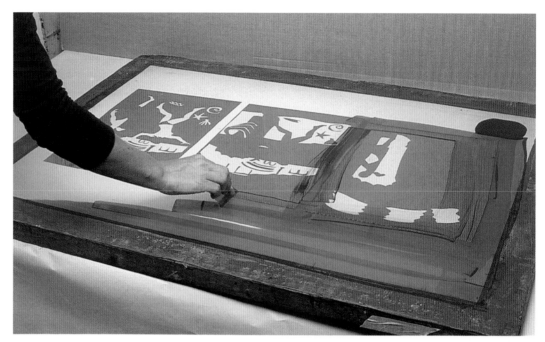

9 Any errors on the stencil can be blocked out in the same way. Here the artist fills in a shape that is not intended to appear in the colour that this stencil will be printing.

Printing technique

1 This demonstration shows printing on a screen frame attached to a vacuum-bed printing table. The screen is securely locked into the frame. The lowered screen does not quite lie flush with the bed – a small gap, known as 'the snap', allows for the 'give' in the screen mesh when the squeegee passes over.

2 The plastic backing on the stencils must be removed before they can be used to print. Take hold of one edge and peel the backing off smoothly.

3 Tape the edges of the screen all round to form a reservoir for the ink and ensure that no colour bleeds under the mesh where it joins the screen frame. You can use gummed paper tape or self-adhesive tape.

4 If you have more than one stencil on the screen, use paper to cover those not printing at this stage. This keeps them clean and prevents ink bleeding through beyond the borders of the first stencil.

5 You need to put registration marks on the screen bed so the image is correctly positioned on the paper. The artist uses the original working sketch to locate the printing area.

6 The sketch is moved around until it is accurately aligned with the stencil image. This picture shows the screen lowered and the artist checking the alignment through the mesh.

7 When the paper is in the correct position, the left-hand lower corner and edge are marked with pieces of masking tape stuck to the screen bed. The printing paper will be positioned against these guides each time the first colour is printed.

8 Mix your ink colours in sufficient quantity to allow for the required number of prints. Screenprinting ink is a thick liquid and is commonly mixed in waxed-paper cups; any leftovers can be stored this way.

9 Pour the ink in an even flow across the bottom border of the screen, below the image. It puddles outwards but, because it is viscous, does not flow into the stencil area.

Stage proof: one

Stage proof: two

Stage proof: three

10 Lift the screen slightly and use the squeegee to push the ink back across the mesh, flooding the colour into the image area.

11 Position the clean piece of printing paper on the screen bed, aligned to the register marks previously taped in place. Lower the screen over the paper.

12 Place the squeegee in the layer of ink at the top of the screen and pull it firmly and evenly across the image area. You must use a squeegee that covers the whole width of the stencil, and keep it firmly horizontal as you pull.

Stage proof: four

Stage proof: five

Stage proof: six

▲ Stage proofs

This sequence shows how the image develops new form and depth with each colour printing. Notice, in the second stage, that the overprinting of transparent yellow on pink has produced a 'mixed' colour – a warm orange. Although each stencil image consists of hard-edged shapes, the artist has successfully achieved a free, lively style of image by using small shapes and patterns to break up the broad colour areas. She keeps the final, black printing very linear, to sharpen the detail.

Registering overprintings
1 To register the second and subsequent colours quickly and accurately, the artist uses an acetate sheet attached to the screen bed on one side. The single colour is printed on the acetate. Then the print is placed underneath.

2 The print is moved around until it aligns exactly with the newly printed colour on the acetate. Then the positions of the bottom corner and left-hand edge are marked with tapes on the screen bed, as before.

Paper stencils

Using newsprint or tracing paper for your stencils is ideal for the beginner in one respect – it enables you to experiment inexpensively. However, remember that a paper stencil is naturally less durable than film. You can draw direct on paper or trace from an original drawing and cut with a knife or scissors. The paper pieces laid on the screen bed adhere to the mesh with the first pass of squeegee and ink, so you do not need to have links between all the shapes. 'Floating' pieces must be positioned carefully at the start, but will then become self-adhesive.

Even if you keep to a fairly simple design you can create exciting variations by trying different ways of inking. Colour blends and variations are easy to form on a screen. This demonstration also shows the use of talcum powder to obtain a mottled texture: the talc is pressed into the mesh at the first inking and forms a block in the same way as a sheet material or liquid filler.

2 Position the printing paper on the screen bed and mark the corner. Lay the paper stencil over it in the required position. You can put pieces of double-sided tape at the corners to help the stencil fix to the screen.

Paper stencil

1 A simple design is freely cut from newsprint, a starburst with an animal figure inside. You can use freestanding shapes within a paper screen stencil, as each piece individually adheres to the screen mesh.

3 Lay out the ink along the bottom of the screen. To make a blend of colours, pour a small pool of each colour and let them flow gently together.

4 Lift the screen and flood the colour back into the mesh by pushing the squeegee upwards. Then lower the screen and pull the other way to make the print.

8 It is easy and economical to experiment using these techniques. This example has been printed using the discarded section cut out of the previous stencil. The giraffe appears this time as a positive image, while the starburst is the negative shape.

5 The starburst shape and the cutout of the giraffe can be seen sticking to the underside of the mesh, while their silhouettes are clearly printed on the paper in the warm colour blend.

6 To add texture using talcum powder, make a paper stencil outlining the shape to be printed and attach it to the screen. Shake talc freely but loosely onto the print.

7 Lower the screen and print the required colour in the usual way. The movement of the squeegee presses the talc into the screen mesh, acting as a block to the ink. This forms a random, lacy pattern.

Filler stencils

Painting on the screen mesh with liquid filler is a satisfyingly direct way of working, enabling you to produce more free and painterly effects. The main drawback for the inexperienced printmaker is that the design has to be worked out negatively – the brushmarks create the non-printing areas. However, because you can see through the screen mesh, you can place a working drawing underneath to guide you as you paint the stencil image; then it is only a matter of concentration.

This demonstration sequence also shows how effectively you can utilise overprintings of semi-transparent colours. The artist uses the process printing colours – cyan (blue), magenta (red) and yellow – with a final overprinting in white. She achieves dark tones such as green and purple, as well as tints of pale blue and pink. This is the same principle as applied in commercial printing, where variable combinations of the process colours achieve an almost infinite colour range – for example, the colour photographs in this book are printed using only cyan, magenta, yellow and black.

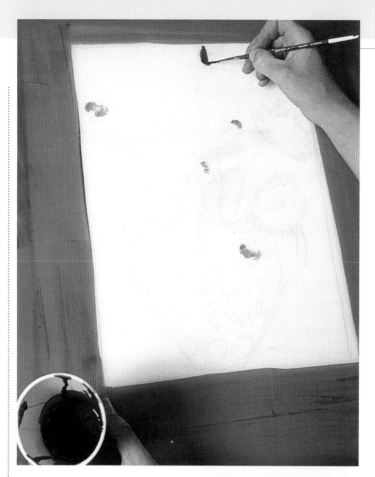

Using filler
1 When painting the filler directly onto the screen mesh, you may find it easiest to place a working drawing or sketch under the mesh as a guide, as shown here.

2 In this example, the artist begins with a stencil that will print blue. To allow for overprintings that will form mixed hues, only the flowers and outline pattern on the vase are blocked out.

Stage proof: one
The first printing (far left) shows broad areas of fairly solid, uniform colour with little detail visible at this stage.

Stage proof: two
Where the red has overprinted on the original blue (left), a rich, deep blue-purple is formed that gives depth and weight to the image. Flashes of the white paper remain where the mesh has been blocked out on both stencils.

1

2

3 The second colour to be printed is red. Only those areas to remain pure blue are blocked out. The artist applies a sponged texture to the foreground area.

4 The background will remain blue and is fully blocked out, leaving the shapes of the flowers, vase and tabletop to print in red.

5 The same process is applied to preparing and printing the third stage of the image – the transparent yellow layer.

7 The white ink is flooded onto the screen and the print is pulled by drawing the squeegee downwards.

6 White ink will be used in the last stage, to vary the tones and enhance the textures. The artist prepares the final stencil exactly, by working to the existing print, placed underneath the screen.

3 **4**

Stage proof: three

The yellow overprints on both the blue and red, producing green and scarlet respectively (far left). This completely transforms not only the colour balance of the image but also the description of the shapes.

Stage proof: four

The white ink of the final stage creates paler tones of all the original colours, and where it is printed over red and blue, it makes a neutral, warm grey (left). Using only four colours, the artist has produced a wide range of hues and tones and some fascinating textures.

2 Wash the ink out of the stencil with the appropriate solvent. In this demonstration, oil-based ink is being cleaned off with white spirit.

3 When printing from one stencil is complete, it can be cleaned out of the screen mesh. Here, water-based filler is flushed out with a spray jet: the screen stands upright in a purpose-made trough. Stubborn traces of filler can be scrubbed away with a soft brush.

Cleaning the screen

1 Between each printing you must clear the screen of ink. Use the squeegee to collect excess ink into a puddle, then pick it up on a palette knife.

Tusche method

Preparing stencils by the tusche method is similar to the filler method, but there is one crucial difference – this is a resist technique which produces a 'positive' stencil. The image is drawn up with tusche (drawing ink) and/or lithographic crayon, both of which are oil-based materials with a greasy texture.

The finished drawing on the screen mesh is coated with gum arabic and is allowed to dry. This acts to block the mesh, as does blue filler, but does not adhere to the tusche. The image is then washed out with white spirit, but the gum arabic, being water-soluble, remains in place. The open areas of the stencil are now those marks that you originally drew and painted, so that the printed image is a positive reading of what was first applied.

Using tusche
1 Work directly on the screen with tusche, using any typical painting techniques. This picture shows spattering applied with a toothbrush between paper masks, after parts of the image have been drawn with a paintbrush.

2 Lithographic crayon can also be used to give a different quality of line. Technically, it acts on the screen mesh in the same way as the tusche. To make the first stencil you can draw quite freely, or follow a working sketch or painted study if you prefer.

3 Allow the painting on the mesh to dry out completely before moving on to the next stage. To save a long wait, you can use a hairdryer to speed up this process.

4 Spread a thin layer of gum arabic over the whole image area. Use a small rectangle of card or plastic to help coat the mesh quickly and evenly. Allow the gum to dry.

Stage proof: one
The first printed image has a fresh, painterly quality with interestingly varied textures. The rough shading of the sea was made by a frottage technique, placing the mesh over a board, then rubbing over it with the litho crayon.

5 Wash out the tusche image with white spirit applied with a rag or sponge. This has no effect on the gum arabic, so you are left with a gummed stencil consisting of the negative areas of your drawing; therefore, it is the positive marks that will print.

Finished print
Second or subsequent colours can be printed by preparing stencils in the same way, using the original print or your working sketch as a guide. The mid-toned green and pale flesh tint applied here maintain a bright, airy quality appropriate to the subject, while overprinting on the left-hand side introduces an effect of deep shadow.

Drypoint

■ DRAWING ON THE PLATE

Because it is the simplest and most direct of the intaglio processes, drypoint is an interesting introduction to working on metal, especially if you have limited access to printmaking facilities. The technique consists of scratching into the surface of a metal plate using a strong, sharp point. The point is used to score the surface, which causes a ridge of metal – called the burr – to be thrown up on one or both sides of the line. This burr holds more ink than the relatively shallow scratches and contributes a velvety, rich quality to the impression.

Drawing on the plate with the point is directly comparable to drawing on paper, though you must use sufficient pressure to mark the metal effectively. But it is an informal process, immediately accessible to anyone with some drawing ability. Its main disadvantage in comparison with other intaglio printmaking methods is that the burrs wear down quickly under the normal actions of inking the plate and passing it through the press, so the number of good-quality prints that can be taken is limited.

Drypoint equipment
1 Combined drypoint needle and burnisher; **2** drypoint needle; **3** combined scraper and burnisher; **4** zinc and copper plates.

Drawing on the plate

Tools and materials

The only materials needed are a plate and a point. Copper or zinc plates are commonly used. Zinc, being a softer metal, is easier to work but produces fewer good impressions. For the drawing tool, a hard steel needle or scriber with a smooth, unfaceted point is generally adequate; the alternative is a point made of precious stone such as diamond.

Because of the relative fragility of the drypoint image, working proofs that allow you to check the progress of the drawing must be kept to a minimum. The plate can be prepared without access to any studio facilities.

Any of the effects associated with line drawing can be expressed through drypoint. You can vary line qualities by altering the pressure and angle of the tool, using the point to score or pick at the metal. The burr is raised most consistently by holding the tool upright or at a steep angle; if the point goes in at too shallow an angle there is a danger that it may undercut the burr and lose the richness of the line.

The character of the drawing can rely mainly on outline or contour, but if you want to introduce tonal areas you can do so by means of conventional drawing techniques such as hatching and crosshatching with close-set parallel lines, or a form of stippling achieved with short, stabbing marks. However, the final state of the print need not depend solely on the positive marks made by the point; you can also use a scraper or burnisher to remove the burr, thus lightening up an area that has been overworked.

Printing technique
To print drypoint, see Intaglio printing, pages 102–109.

1 Start to draw on the plate with the needle as you would with a pencil on paper. It is easiest to sketch out a few faint guidelines first, then gradually strengthen the lines and develop the textures.

Finished print
The first prints from the finished plate (right) have a very rich tone, with dense blacks on the darker cat. This is due to the heavy burr created by the stippled marks. After several impressions, you can see how the dark tones have faded (far right) as the burr wears down in printing – individual marks are visible on the cat's back. Altogether ten acceptable prints were taken from this plate.

2 Changing the angle of the tool enables you to create more or less burr on the line, while more pressure gives you increased thickness. Try to vary the line qualities expressively, according to the details of your subject.

4 ▶ Once the design is fully drawn out, take a proof to check the image. In this example (right), the shapes are judged to be satisfactory, but the tones are not yet rich enough.

3 You can create greyed areas by hatching blocks of fine parallel lines. The closer the lines and the more burred the marks, the heavier the tonal emphasis will be.

5 The drawing is worked much more heavily on the plate with hatched and stippled textures. A second proof is taken (right) as work on the plate nears completion and, using this as a guide, some unwanted lines are smoothed out with the burnisher.

Mezzotint

■ ROCKING THE PLATE

■ SCRAPING AND BURNISHING

Mezzotint is an unusual intaglio process in two respects. Preparation of the plate requires quite intense physical labour; and the image is worked light out of dark, a reversal of typical approaches in drawing and printmaking. Before any creative work can begin, the plate surface is systematically roughened to produce an overall texture that prints as an even, dense black. Mid-tones and whites are retrieved by smoothing out this texture to varying degrees.

The tonal emphasis gives mezzotint prints a soft, often atmospheric quality with minimal linear structure. The technique was invented primarily as a reproduction process that would provide a more painterly effect than line engraving, allowing subtly fluid gradation of tone. It has not been consistently exploited as a creative medium in its own right, and the tedious, purely mechanical aspect of 'rocking' the plate to achieve the initial tone can be a deterrent. However, the character of the mezzotint impression is unique, and the transition to pale tones, even high whites, out of intense, rich darks can have great dramatic impact.

Tools and materials

Copper plate is used for mezzotint, and a mezzotint rocker, a broad chisel-like implement with a curved, toothed blade, is the tool used to create the rough ground. The teeth indent the plate surface and throw up a burr. To achieve a consistent texture, the rocker has to be moved gradually all over the plate in all directions, and a rocking pole is often used to assist the action. Rockers are made in several sizes with differently spaced teeth – fine, closely set teeth give the most consistent tone, while a coarse rocker creates more burr and therefore provides the densest blacks, but with a less even texture overall. If you wish to try out the effect of mezzotint without having to do the hard work of preparation you can obtain pre-rocked plates. These are mechanically prepared, with an even texture; however, they are expensive.

The process of 'drawing' on the plate – bringing back the lighter tones – involves removing or smoothing down the burr using a scraper and burnisher. To rework an area where you have taken out too much of the tone, you can use a roulette – a small, serrated wheel set in a handle, which can be rolled across the plate to enhance detail or repair the ground. Roulettes are available in different shapes and sizes.

1

2

5

4

Mezzotint equipment
1 Coarse mezzotint rocker; **2** fine mezzotint rocker; **3** copper plate; **4** burnisher; **5** curved scraper.

3

Rocking the plate

The reason why rocking the plate is such a laborious process is that it must be done quite consistently in several different directions – first at right angles to the sides of the plate, then along diagonal paths from the edges. The time it takes depends partly on the size of the plate in relation to the width of the rocker; a very large plate may take days to prepare.

A grid of parallel lines is drawn up to guide the tool, which is held upright on the surface and rocked from side to side on the curved blade, at the same time moving gradually forwards along the grid lines. When the rocker is hand-held, the movement comes from the forearm and wrist rather than just the hand. The weighted rocking pole relieves some of the strain of this action by contributing a consistent pressure and keeping the tool on a straight path.

Using the rocker
1 If you are working on a large plate, using a rocking pole helps to lighten the physical effort of rocking the texture initially. The weighted pole can be supported on a frame that allows it to rock easily while keeping a consistent direction, or it can be rested on the work surface.

2 Grasp the pole right behind the point where the rocker is attached and rock it steadily from side to side, at the same time gradually pushing it forwards across the plate.

3 You can alternatively rock without the pole, which puts more pressure on your forearm. The plate must be rocked in many different directions to obtain a dense texture, indicated by the grid lines visible here.

Scraping and burnishing

Individual or combined processes of scraping and burnishing can be used to develop the variation of tones. The scraper removes the burr and the burnisher polishes the surface; to work back to pure white, both tools must be used. Intermediate greys can be formed by scraping and burnishing to different degrees or just by using the burnisher to flatten the burr gently. The only way of finding out the extent and degree of either action required for a particular effect is through experience.

To give yourself a layout for the design, you can start by drawing on the roughened plate with a soft pencil. You can also rub ink into the plate so that you are working on a black surface, which helps you to estimate the effect of the scraping and burnishing. If you do this, clean off the ink each time you stop work or it will dry hard and you may damage the burr of the plate while trying to remove it. Keep proofing to a minimum, as the printing process gradually wears down the texture.

Drawing on the plate
1 Guidelines for the design can be drawn on the metal using a soft pencil. Where a sharp outline is needed, draw into the rocked texture with a metal scriber.

2 The curved tip of a burnisher flattens the burr on the metal plate. The shaded area will print as a light tone, graduating to dark as it recedes from the outline.

3 You can work with a scraper to clear very pale-toned areas quickly. This has a less delicate effect than a burnisher: it is a matter of personal preference which to use, according to the character of the design.

▲ **PHILIP COOMBS**
DOLL'S HEAD (MEZZOTINT)
The graded tones of mezzotint have an almost photographic quality when applied to heavily modelled shapes. The strong black of the fully rocked texture, as seen in the background of this image, has a rich, velvety intensity.

Printing technique
To print mezzotints, see Intaglio printing, pages 102–109.

Etching

- **PREPARING THE PLATE**

- **APPLYING HARD GROUND**

- **DRAWING ON THE PLATE**

- **BITING THE PLATE**

- **AQUATINT**

- **SOFT-GROUND ETCHING**

- **SUGAR-LIFT PROCESS**

- **ETCHED TEXTURES**

The essential difference between etching techniques and the other intaglio methods is that the marks are not achieved by incising or scraping the metal. The image is developed by corroding the metal plate with acid, using acid-resistant grounds to protect the areas not to be etched.

Etching is a remarkably versatile and expressive area of printmaking. Different ways of manipulating the grounds, the mark-making processes, the action and extent of the corrosion, and the printing process give the artist an infinite range of creative opportunities.

Tools and materials

To produce even the most basic etched impression you will need quite a wide range of materials and equipment, and it is essential to learn the techniques under supervision in a properly equipped studio. Safety factors are particularly important. At various stages the plate has to be heated on a hotplate or burner, and the process of etching involves using an acid bath which should be sited well away from other work areas and must be well ventilated to remove fumes.

The simplest range of etching equipment consists of a metal plate, acid-resistant ground and varnish, an etching needle and an acid bath. Copper or zinc plates are usually chosen, although steel and other metals are also suitable. Copper gives more refined effects of line and tone and, being harder, stands up better to the wear and tear of printing. But zinc (or a zinc-like alloy offered by some suppliers) is a perfectly adequate and less expensive material on which to learn the craft.

Etching grounds are either hard or soft. The hard ground is the standard one for line etching, while the soft ground (see pages 96–97) creates different, particular surface effects. Both are available in solid cake form, and are melted onto the plate and spread with a dabber or roller. Alternatively, a liquid hard ground can be used. Stopping-out varnish is an acid-resistant liquid applied to reinforce the ground in areas not to be etched – or to cover up exposed metal.

1

2

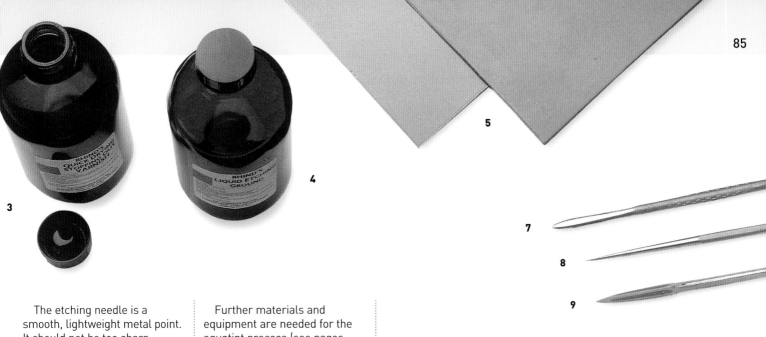

The etching needle is a smooth, lightweight metal point. It should not be too sharp because it is important that it does not scratch the metal as you draw into the ground. It is advisable to obtain a purpose-made tool, but you can improvise with a darning needle attached firmly to a pen or brush handle. The type and strength of acid solution, or mordant, depends on the metal being used and the intensity of the corrosive effect required (see pages 92–93).

Further materials and equipment are needed for the aquatint process (see pages 94–95) and for printing the plate, but the basic method of printing for all intaglio images is the same. If you use a professionally equipped etching studio, either for commercial hire or as part of an educational institution, it will have all the facilities you need for any of the techniques described here.

Etching equipment
1 Hard ground; **2** soft ground; **3** stopping-out varnish; **4** liquid hard ground; **5** zinc and copper plates; **6** leather-covered dabber; **7** burnisher; **8** etching needle; **9** scraper; **10** feathers for clearing acid bubbles from plate; **11** clamp for holding plate during smoking.

See also
Biting the plate, pages 92–93;
Aquatint, pages 94–95;
Soft-ground etching, pages 96–97

Preparing the plate

The intaglio (sunken) areas of an etching plate can be quite deep, in some cases both deep and narrow, and so the print has to be taken under heavy pressure. Because the paper is forced into the sunken areas it becomes embossed to some extent, as well as picking up the ink. If the plate has hard, vertical edges, these can cut through the paper under pressure, even though the thickness of the metal is no more than 2–4mm ($1/16$–$1/8$in). To avoid damage to the paper and the soft blankets that help to spread the pressure of the press rollers, the edges of the plate are bevelled to an angle of about 45 degrees by rubbing them down with a file. This is usually done as a preliminary process, although edges can also be filed and polished immediately prior to printing.

Before laying the acid-resistant ground the surface must be clean and completely free of grease, otherwise the ground may adhere imperfectly and cause an effect known as 'foul-biting' in the acid, when blemishes allow non-printing areas of the plate to become mildly and irregularly corroded.

Bevelling the plate
1 Position the plate so that it is firmly supported, but one edge just protrudes from the edge of the work surface. File all along the edge, keeping the file at an angle of 45 degrees. Repeat on all sides of the plate.

2 To smooth any marks that the file has left, work along the bevelled edges with a scraper, held at the same angle. Shave the metal lightly with the scraper blade.

Printing technique
To print etchings, see Intaglio printing, pages 102–109.

3 You can leave mitred corners or round them off completely. Because intaglio prints have a slightly embossed effect, the edges of the plate do leave a clear impression on the paper, so they should be even and clean.

Degreasing

1 Put a small heap of French chalk or whiting on the plate and pour in a few drops of household ammonia.

2 Work the ammonia and chalk into a paste and rub it across the whole plate surface, using a lightweight scrubbing brush, cotton wool or a soft rag.

3 Rinse off the plate with clean water. If it is completely degreased, the water will flow evenly across the surface. If the water runs around remaining grease spots, repeat the process. Then dry off the plate.

Applying hard ground

The ground must be applied evenly to form an effective acid-resistant coating that is durable but can be lifted easily and cleanly as you draw into it with the etching needle. The solid ball of hard ground as you buy it from the supplier is shiny and brown-black. The basic ingredients are bitumen, wax and rosin (colophony), but there are various recipes and some etchers prefer to make their own. It is applied to a warmed plate, heated gently on a hotplate. Dabs of ground melt onto the surface of the metal and are rolled out in all directions to form a smooth, thin coating. The completed ground is a warm, golden-brown colour.

It is important not to 'overcook' the ground, as too much heat causes it first to slide on the surface, then to coagulate and stick to the applicator so that the coating becomes lumpy and uneven. If this happens, cool the plate, clean it off and start again. Getting the right touch in grounding a plate is a matter of practice; for instance, you may find a forwards pass of the roller lays down the coating, and a quick backwards roll lifts any excess.

Smoking

Smoking the ground with tapers, which hardens it slightly and turns it a darker colour, is not essential, but it does make it easier to see the marks of your drawing with the needle. Wax tapers are used, which give off a dark smoke that deposits carbon on the ground. Only the smoky trail from the tapers, not the naked flame, should touch the ground, which turns black and shiny as it carbonises. Using the centre of the flame can scorch the ground, and it will begin to flake.

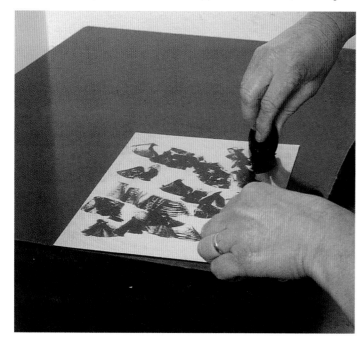

Applying hard ground
1 Put the degreased plate on the hotplate and let it warm through. Dab the ball of hard ground onto the surface, allowing it to melt into random smears.

2 Use a hard-wearing roller to spread the ground evenly across the plate, working in all directions.

3 Continue to work with the roller, travelling from side to side both ways on the plate, until the ground is thin and even, and a uniform golden-brown colour.

Smoking the ground
Secure the plate at one edge in a pair of pliers or hand-held clamp. Put a small fold of paper at the edge to prevent the tool marking the plate surface. Light three or four tapers twisted together to make a long flame. Move the flame under the plate in a circling motion, so that only the smoke trail from the tapers touches the ground. Continue until the ground darkens all over.

Drawing on the plate

Once the ground has been smoked and allowed to cool you are ready to start drawing. If you wish to put down guidelines, you can draw on the ground with a soft, blunted pencil or trace down your design using transfer paper. However, the point of any print process is to exploit the characteristics of the materials and methods, so don't try to copy a preparatory drawing too slavishly – let the composition evolve freely on the plate.

You can manipulate the etching needle in just the same ways as you would a pencil or pen. The important thing to remember is that it need only lift the ground – it is actually a disadvantage if it scratches into the metal – so do not apply too much pressure. The work of cutting into the metal is all done by the acid, and if your lines are unevenly scored into the plate, this will affect the quality of the acid bite. You do need to expose the plate cleanly, however; if you can still see a thin brown film across the line the ground is not fully removed.

You will gradually get used to the effects of etching and learn the best ways to draw up your image. A very broad line will bite as a shallow furrow in the metal, and because of the surface quality of the intaglio and the method of inking and wiping the plate for printing, this will print paler at the centre than at the edges. In hatched areas where lines are close together the acid may break through the tiny sections of ground dividing them. If you wish to begin with fairly even, black line work, keep the drawing relatively fine and the textures clean and distinct.

Stopping out

Before etching, every part of the plate surface that is not deliberately exposed as part of the image to be etched must be completely protected by an acid-resistant covering. This involves painting the back and the bevelled edges of the plate with stopping-out varnish – the plate may have been supplied with a prepared acid resist backing, but the edges must still be stopped out.

On the front of the plate, any part of the ground where there is no drawing can be covered with varnish to prevent foul-biting. You can also use stopping-out varnish to refine lines scratched too coarsely in the ground or to cover errors.

Drawing on the plate
1 If you are transferring an existing design to the plate, cover it with transfer or carbon paper and lay a trace of your drawing on top.

2 Tape down one edge of the trace so that it is anchored in position. Go over the drawing with a pencil so the transfer paper lays down the lines on the ground beneath.

3 You can draw directly into the ground with an etching needle as freely as you would draw on paper. Avoid scratching into the surface of the metal. The lines you make should just lift the ground cleanly.

Stopping out
When the drawing on the ground is complete, paint stopping-out varnish over any non-printing areas where the ground is imperfect. Finally, stop out the edges and back of the plate as necessary, so no bare metal will be exposed to the acid except in the drawing.

Alternative tools
1 You can use other implements to work into the ground. An ordinary dip pen makes calligraphic, double lines because of the split in the nib.

2 A small roulette – this is a dentist's drill bit – rolled over the ground makes a lightly toothed linear pattern.

Biting the plate

The action of acid on metal is called the 'bite'. One of the difficulties for the beginner is that there are no simple rules for estimating how long the plate needs to be in the acid bath. The speed and strength of the bite varies according to a number of factors – the types of metal and acid used, the extent of plate surface exposed to acid, and the temperature of the acid bath and that of the studio environment. You also have to consider the effect you wish to achieve – whether the lines should be fine and shallow-bitten or deep and strong. This is all learned by experience, but even so it remains a relatively unpredictable technique.

A plate can be bitten in stages to produce different line qualities. All the lines are bitten for a certain length of time, then the plate is removed from the acid, rinsed and dried, the fine lines are covered with stopping-out varnish and the plate is returned to the acid to etch the remaining lines more deeply. A detailed image may require many different stages of grounding and biting. It is difficult, though not impossible, to rework bitten lines cleanly through a new ground. The addition of tone and texture may, however, alter the effect of the initial line work, and decisions about reworking can be made on the basis of proofs pulled at different stages.

The acid bath
The bath to contain the acid solution can be a glass, porcelain or plastic dish or tray – obviously the material must not be susceptible to the corrosive effect. Ideally it should be sited under an extractor hood; at the least it must stand in a well-ventilated part of the studio. When checking a plate in the acid, do not stand over the bath for too long, because you will be breathing in fumes.

It is essential to work carefully and steadily when handling acid bottles and mixing solutions. Preferably this will be done for you by an experienced tutor or technician. Acid and water generate heat when combined, so to control this, the acid must be added to the water, never vice versa. The solution for the acid bath, which varies from a 1:1 ratio to about 10:1 water to acid, depending upon the purpose, is safer to work with than full-strength acid, but you should still take precautions like wearing rubber gloves, and if any of the solution splashes on your skin, rinse it off with clean water.

For copper and zinc plates, nitric acid can be used. The solution is made slightly stronger for copper, which bites slowly, and the reaction with the metal gradually turns the acid blue. On zinc, the acid bites quite quickly and produces bubbles on the plate surface. These must be removed with a soft brush or feather; otherwise the bubbles form a sort of acid-resist and the result is a textured bite.

Two other solutions commonly used are Dutch mordant for copper – a mixture of hydrochloric acid, potassium chlorate and water – and ferric chloride, used for copper or zinc. Be sure to get professional advice on the type of mordant to use and its strength for the job in hand.

Biting the plate
1 Lower the plate gently into the acid bath. In the parts of this process when your fingers are likely to be in contact with the acid, it is wise to wear rubber gloves.

2 As the acid begins to act on the metal, you will see bubbles forming on the plate. Brush them away gently with a feather.

3 When the biting is complete, remove the plate from the acid, transfer it to the sink and wash it off with clean running water.

4 Return the plate to the work surface and wipe off the ground and stopping-out varnish with white spirit. When the plate is completely clean, you are ready to take a first-stage proof.

5 A line etching reflects the vitality of your drawing and at the same time contributes qualities of its own – particularly the richness of the black line, due to the amount of ink held in the intaglio. You can produce finished etchings in line work only. This example will be given more overall tone with the addition of aquatint (see overleaf).

Aquatint

This process enables you to create areas of solid tone on an etching plate and gradations of tone from white through a range of greys to black. It is commonly combined with line etching to give weight and modelling to the image, but can be used as the primary technique.

Aquatint involves laying a coating of resin dust on the plate, which is then heated, causing the resin to melt into tiny globules. On removal from the heat, these harden and when the plate is etched the acid eats into the pits between the globules to produce a fine, all-over intaglio texture. Tonal variations are made by successive stages of stopping out areas of the plate and biting the exposed shapes in the acid, gradually etching the pitted surface more deeply. To check the tones, the resin must be removed with solvent before proofing the plate, so you cannot rebite into the same texture after proofing.

Areas which are too dark can be retrieved by burnishing, although this affects the texture. You can also use aquatint as a dark-to-light method, like mezzotint, by biting a continuous dark tone over the whole plate and working into it with a scraper and burnisher.

Applying aquatint resin

There are several ways of doing this, and the choice will depend on the facilities available and the textural effect you wish to produce. A dense, even aquatint tone is best achieved by using a purpose-designed aquatint box. This is fitted with bellows or a revolving paddle worked from outside, with which you agitate the resin dust in the box so that it flies up in a dense cloud. The plate is then inserted face up and the dust allowed to settle on it.

The alternative is to apply the resin direct to the plate with some kind of shaker. Various devices can be used – a muslin bag; a salt shaker; a jar with muslin stretched across the top; a fine sieve. The more random and uncontrollable the fall of resin from the shaker, the more irregular the aquatint texture. A rough aquatint can be effective in prints that incorporate textural variety, but if you are looking for subtle tonal gradations, the resin must be finely and evenly laid.

Biting an aquatint

Appreciable variations of tone occur in minutes, even seconds, as you go through successive bitings. At the first stage, you stop out (see page 91) the areas of the plate to remain white, and also cover the back and edges of the plate with varnish. The acid solution should not be too strong, or it may eat sideways under the resin rather than etching down evenly into the pitted texture. After the first biting remove the plate from the acid, then rinse and dry it. Then stop out the next lightest tone and return the plate briefly to the acid.

This process is continued until you have as many tones as you require. The accumulated time that the plate is in the acid may be less than an hour over all, but you need time in between for stopping out. The varnish must cover the aquatint grain thickly and cleanly, and be allowed to dry completely before the plate is rebitten. Be careful not to leave the plate too long in the acid on the final bite, or it may break down the resin ground, resulting in a foul-bitten, irregular texture.

If you have begun with line etching, your line work will provide a guide for laying in the aquatint tones. If you are working direct onto aquatint ground, you can trace down a layout using transfer paper.

Applying aquatint resin
1 The easiest and most reliable way to lay aquatint is in a purpose-made box, fitted with a revolving paddle. The box contains a large amount of resin which, when the box is not in use, settles in the bottom of the drum (see diagram below).

A Stirring up resin dust

B Inserting etching plate

C Allowing dust to settle

2 Close up the front of the box and turn the handle vigorously. This turns the paddle which agitates the resin dust and causes it to fly up inside the drum (see diagram A).

3 Lock the handle in the position where it keeps the interior paddle horizontal. Put your etching plate on a wire tray and insert it in the box. A face mask prevents you from inhaling any dust that drifts out. Close up the front of the box again (see diagram B).

4 After a few minutes, check that an even coating of resin has fallen onto the plate (see diagram C), then remove the plate from the tray and transfer it to a metal grid. Use a small blowtorch or Bunsen burner to heat the plate from underneath.

5 Keep the heat source moving gently underneath the plate so that it does not scorch the resin. The whitish, powdery coating gradually melts and turns yellow. When this colour has spread right across the plate, allow it to cool.

Aquatint tones
You can stop out areas of the design and return the plate to the acid several times to produce a range of tones, but overbiting may break down the aquatint. In this example, there are three greys – pale, mid-toned and dark – and the heavier black. Pale grey might require only seconds in the acid, black several minutes in all. The tonal modelling can considerably alter the character of the print – compare this version with the line etching on page 93.

See also
Stopping out, page 91

Soft-ground etching

Soft ground is similar in composition to hard ground but has a higher grease content that contributes the softer texture. It is applied to the plate in the same way as hard ground (see pages 88–89), using a roller or dabber to spread the coating evenly and thinly. A soft ground is not smoked.

You can draw directly into soft ground with an etching needle to produce a line drawing with a softer, less precise character than that typical of work on hard ground. However, where soft ground really comes into its own is in using techniques that depend upon making an impression in the ground.

Because the coating is soft and tacky, it is picked up by any material pressed down hard against it. You can draw through a piece of paper onto the ground to produce a line quality resembling soft pencil or crayon marks. All sorts of found materials leave a clear impression that etches quite accurately – woven fabrics, yarns and meshes, feathers, thin wood-grain. To make the impression, the material is laid on the plate, covered with a clean sheet of paper and rolled through the press.

2 Use a hard but not sharp point to impress on the paper. Here the artist is working with a plastic knitting needle.

Soft-ground textures
1 To make a drawing on soft ground, either work direct onto a clean piece of paper laid over the plate, or make a master drawing beforehand that you can trace over.

3 At any stage of the drawing you can lift the paper to check the impression on the plate, but be sure to keep one side of the paper firmly anchored, so it goes back down in exactly the same place.

4 When using found materials to create soft-ground textures, simply lay the pieces on the plate in the appropriate position.

5 It is worth experimenting with all kinds of materials – some textures 'take' better than others. This example shows tracing paper, scrim, Cellophane, string, ribbon, wadding and dried leaves from the onions that are the subject of the print.

9 The final result of this print is a very pleasing combination of tones and textures. Although the materials were quite randomly chosen, they suit the subject well and the contrast of soft lines and tonal masses gives the image weight and depth.

6 Move the plate to the bed of the press and cover it with a clean sheet of paper. Run it through the press so that the pressure embeds the materials firmly in the ground.

7 Lift the materials from the plate very carefully, without actually touching the ground. You can pick up paper or fibrous materials with an etching needle, or catch one end with tweezers.

8 Stop out any non-printing areas of the plate and protect the back and edges as necessary. You can now etch the plate in acid – keep checking the action of the acid bite, so that fragile textures do not break down.

See also
Applying hard ground, pages 88–89

Sugar-lift process

This process is generally associated with aquatint, but can also be used to expose areas of the plate for open biting. (This term simply means exposing a broad area of the plate surface to acid, as compared to line work or the grainy texture of aquatint.) Usually, when you use stopping-out varnish to protect unexposed areas, you are painting it on as a negative surround to the shapes that will be bitten. The sugar-lift process is a resist technique that enables you to etch any shape that you have painted positively, from a solid, flat area to a textured brushmark.

You paint your design on the plate with a sugar solution coloured with ink or gouache, allow it to dry, and cover it with diluted stopping-out varnish or liquid hard ground. You then immerse the plate in warm water, and the sugar gradually dissolves and lifts the varnish, leaving the acid-resistant coating in place around the painted marks. You can then aquatint the exposed areas or etch them as they are.

Sugar-lift process

1 Paint your design with the sugar solution on a clean, degreased plate. The solution used here was one part sugar to four parts water and one part ink. Heat the water to dissolve the sugar grains.

2 Allow the sugar painting to dry completely – this can take some time, especially if the atmosphere is humid as the sugar reabsorbs moisture. When dry, cover the whole plate with a thin coat of stopping-out varnish diluted with white spirit.

3 When the stopping-out varnish has dried, immerse the plate in a bath of water. Leave it until the sugar begins to dissolve and the varnish lifts. Once this happens you can brush it lightly to assist the process.

4 When the sugar coating has all lifted, leaving the design exposed in the varnish layer, place it in acid to bite as required (you can apply aquatint over the varnish if preferred). This plate is open biting – the bubbles show the fast action of the acid on the exposed metal.

5 The resist technique retains the fluid, calligraphic quality of the original painting. Open biting typically produces the strong outlines visible in this print, especially if the plate is etched quite deeply. After the first bite, parts of the image were stopped out and the plate returned to the acid for further biting, which produced the darker tones in the outlines and small shapes.

Etched textures

Etching provides a far greater range of surface effects than any other intaglio process. All the techniques previously described can be combined on one plate, and there is plenty of room for experimentation. For example, stopping-out varnish floated onto water breaks up into fascinating marbled textures that can be transferred to the metal simply by holding the plate face down on the water surface. There are also many variations that can be obtained using different materials to impress a soft ground, or by applying stopping-out varnish to a clean plate using standard painting techniques such as drybrushing and spattering. The strength and depth of the acid bite can also be exploited to vary tone and detail.

You need to plan carefully so that your composition does not become overloaded with busy textures, but since the marks that result from different processes are all etched into a single surface, they generally cohere very well when printed.

Marbling
Stopping-out varnish floated on water picks up on the surface of the plate and etches into this rich, random pattern. The striped effect is caused by open biting between strips painted with stopping-out varnish. The white areas represent the unetched plate surface.

Drawing and impressing
The lines were drawn in the hard ground with free, quick strokes of the etching needle. The rounded smudges are fingerprints, made by pressing on the ground with a fingertip dampened with white spirit.

Rough open bite
This fully exposed area of the plate was left in the acid for a long period. The bubbles building up on the metal due to the action of the acid gradually formed a resist; the bite worked around the bubbles to produce this pebbly texture.

Etching and drypoint
Various areas of etched open bite and linear textures produced an interestingly atmospheric print, but lacked strong contrast. The darkest tone was supplied by raising a burr with a drypoint needle on the zinc plate.

Open bite and aquatint
The spotted pattern was formed by spattering white spirit onto hard ground and blotting with a rag. The dark background is aquatinting; the orange colour a coating of ink rolled over the plate surface.

Soft ground and aquatint
The wood-grain effect was achieved by impressing a thin wood veneer into soft ground. The criss-cross wire pattern was fully stopped out while the wood texture was etched, and was later aquatinted to achieve the tonal variations.

Combined textures
The grid is composed of lines ruled in hard ground, the smoother tonal areas are shallow open biting applied to areas exposed by wiping the ground with white spirit on a rag. The scumbled texture was rubbed into the ground with wire wool. The 'bird's wing' detail was made by drybrushing into the ground with a brush dipped in white spirit.

Intaglio printing

■ PREPARING PAPER

■ INKING AND WIPING

■ TAKING THE PRINT

■ COLOUR PRINTING

The method of printing from an intaglio plate is essentially the same for all processes – drypoint, mezzotint and etching. Unlike block printing or lithography, when it is strictly surface contact that forms the impression, the pressure of printing must force the paper into the intaglio to pick up an even impression from marks as varied as fine creviced lines, delicate aquatinting and deep, open bite. The way the paper is pushed into the lines and sunken areas in the plate produces an embossed effect that adds an extra dimension to the print.

A flat-bed press is used, consisting of a heavy metal bed that passes between two large rollers. Studio presses are usually very heavy and work on a gearing system that makes it easier to move the weight of the bed, operated by turning a large wheel at one side. The space between the rollers can be varied to alter the pressure. Soft felt blankets, which cushion the rollers and spread the pressure evenly, are used to cover the plate and bed before they are pressed through the rollers.

Equipment for intaglio printing
1 Glass mixing slab; **2** tube of intaglio ink; **3** palette knife; **4** coarse and fine wiping canvas (scrim); **5** tinned intaglio ink; **6** powder pigment; **7** copperplate oil; **8** blotting paper and tissue; **9** rollers.

Preparing paper

Intaglio plates are printed on damp paper, which gives more flexibility for pressing into the intaglio without the paper splitting or failing to pick up all the ink. The paper is prepared beforehand by soaking in clean water. It is then drained and blotted, interleaved with blotting paper, pressed between boards, and left until needed.

High-quality watercolour papers are often chosen for intaglio printing, particularly hand-made or mould-made papers with deckle edges which look good when framed without a mount. It is important that the weight and texture of the paper suits the style and complexity of the image, so that fine marks are picked up accurately where appropriate and the qualities of the print do not compete with that of the printing surface.

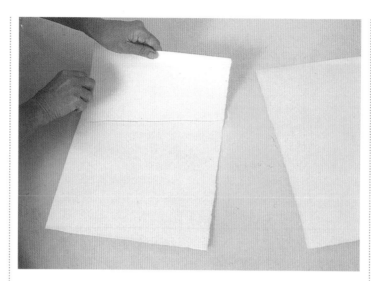

Preparing paper
1 Put the paper to soak in a bath of clean water. The amount of time it needs to soak depends on the weight and texture of the paper – it must become fully damp right through the fibres.

2 Lift the paper from the water bath and let it drain. Lay it on a sheet of blotting paper and cover it with a second sheet. You can build up a stack of paper layers in this way. Lay a board on top to press it so the paper sheets remain flat and moist.

Inking and wiping

Before you start to take a print, make sure the plate is completely clean and free of any traces of ground or varnish. Check that the edges are cleanly bevelled; if they have been damaged during the etching process, file them smooth again.

The inking process requires a heavy first application of ink, which must be rubbed well into the plate so that it is pushed into all the intaglio marks. The plate is then wiped carefully and thoroughly to take off all surplus colour. This is easiest to do if the plate is warmed slightly on a hotplate, but heating is not always essential. It is important that there is no 'loose' ink left on the surface after wiping, as this will prevent the true tones of the intaglio being seen, and make it impossible to produce identical prints.

Mixing ink
1 Use a broad palette knife to lay a heap of powder pigment on the mixing slab. Make a depression in the centre and pour in a small pool of copperplate oil.

Although ready mixed inks are available, many printmakers like to mix up inks from powder pigments and copperplate oil. Selecting particular types of pigments, even different kinds of black, gives them control over the tones and colours of the print as well as the consistency of the ink, which can vary from a rich liquid to a thick paste.

The ink can be applied with a ready-made dabber or simply with a pad of coarse muslin, called scrim or tarlatan. The same muslin is used for wiping, with a slightly finer fabric sometimes chosen for later stages. The final wipe, which polishes the white areas and cleans the pale tones, is done with the heel of the hand, dusted with French chalk, or with pieces of tissue rubbed flatly over the metal surface. Drypoint plates are not hand-wiped, because the burred texture is abrasive.

2 Push the pigment into the oil from all sides and start to work it into a paste, alternately pressing and lifting the mixture with the knife. Continue until the ink has a smooth consistency. The amount of oil you add determines whether it is stiff or fluid.

Inking the plate

1 Let the clean etching plate warm through on the hotplate. Twist a small piece of wiping canvas (scrim) to make a dabber – a little firm pad with a 'stalk' that you can hold it by. Pick up ink on the pad and dab it onto the plate.

2 Work the ink into the intaglio all over the plate surface. Use a generous amount of colour, and push it firmly into any deep lines and heavily bitten areas.

3 Fold a large piece of wiping canvas into a pad and briskly wipe the surface to remove excess ink. Keep the pad travelling flatly across the plate to clean the smoother textures and lighter tones – do not dig the ink out of the deep intaglio.

4 When you can see the design clearly, continue wiping with a clean piece of canvas, working lightly and consistently so no obvious smears of ink are left on the surface. To polish the light tones and obtain a clean tonal range from the aquatint areas, go over the plate with a piece of tissue. Spread your fingers flatly on the tissue and rub with a circular motion.

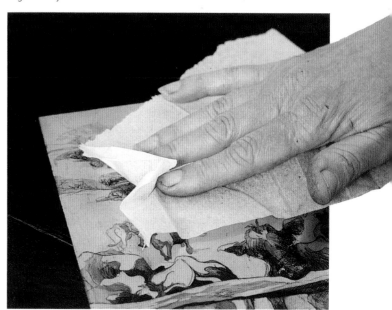

Taking the print

This process is very simple. The plate is positioned on the flat bed of the press and the damp paper laid over the top. The felt blankets are spread over them, between two and five layers, with a lightweight felt next to the plate and a heavy, napped blanket next to the press roller. The handle of the press is turned to run the bed between the rollers.

To make sure that the impression is taken square on the paper, with even borders, you can lay a base sheet of paper on the bed of the press with the outline of the plate marked on it. When the printing paper is placed on the plate, the edges can be aligned to the base sheet, working from one corner. Alternatively, you can stick masking-tape guides for both plate and paper onto the bed of the press.

2 Turn back the board on the paper stack and lift out one sheet of damp paper. To keep the edges clean, hold it between small paper folds.

Taking a print
1 Make sure the blankets are in place on the press, fed in under the roller but turned back so the bed of the press is clear. Lay the inked plate on a clean sheet of paper on the bed.

3 Position one corner of the paper on the press in relation to the inked plate. Gently lower the paper and smooth it down on the plate.

4 Pull the blankets down onto the bed of the press one by one, smoothing them carefully in place over the plate and paper.

5 Turn the handle of the press to pass the bed between the rollers. It should turn easily, though a slightly greater effort is required as the thickness of the plate moves through, as the pressure of the rollers does need to be quite heavy.

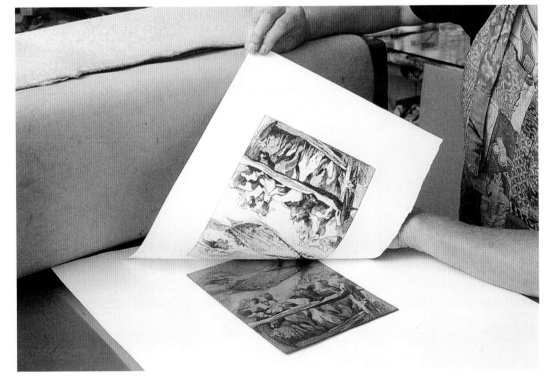

6 Take the bed through far enough to release both the plate and printing paper from beneath the rollers. Turn back the blankets and peel the print up gently from one corner. The finished print is the example shown in full on page 95.

Colour printing

There are several ways of introducing colour into an intaglio printing, even when you are working on only one plate. One method is to ink up the intaglio in one colour, usually black or a dark colour such as blue or sepia, then use a roller to lay down a flat coating of a second colour over the plate surface. Any areas required to print white can be masked off with paper before the colour roll-up.

You can also ink the intaglio in more than one colour, using separate dabbers for different parts of the plate. This is not absolutely precise, as colour areas will merge or overlap slightly in the process of inking and wiping, but it can produce very expressive and atmospheric results.

A more laborious method, which keeps colour areas quite separate, involves cutting up the plate and inking each piece individually. When you come to print, the pieces are then reassembled like a jigsaw on the bed of the press. The disadvantage is that you are likely to see white lines between the cut pieces on the final impression.

Alternatively, you can overprint separate plates, each representing a different part of the design and inked in different colours. This approach needs careful planning, and you have to register the images accurately, both when preparing the plates and when printing.

3 You cannot get hard edges to the colour areas working in this way, but both colours appear distinctly, with a gentle transition of mixed tone between them.

Inking in two colours
1 Warm the clean plate on the hotplate. Make a clean dabber out of wiping canvas and apply your first colour to the appropriate areas. Wipe off the excess.

2 Apply the second colour to the required areas of the plate and wipe off the excess. Wipe again with clean canvas, then finish with tissue as you did before.

▼ LOUISE BIRD
BUMBLEBEES ON ECHINOPS (MEZZOTINT)
Inspired by observing foraging bumblebees, this mezzotint uses the technique of selectively burnishing areas of the plate to create a range of tones to form the image. The plate is then carefully inked, applying colours individually to different areas of the plate. The final result comes from a single print, with only a small amount of colour application to highlight the bees, post printing.

▲ ANJA PERCIVAL
DUSK LIGHT IV (ETCHING)
Drawing with a wax crayon on aquatint results in subtle tonal differences within the artist's imagery. During the printing process ink is applied to the plate in a painterly fashion that allows the artist to vary density and colour in such a way as to exaggerate the effect of the etched image.

Lithography

■ PREPARING THE PLATE

■ PROCESSING THE IMAGE

■ PRINTING

Lithography is in one respect an ideal introduction to printmaking because the image is created by standard drawing and painting techniques, put onto the printing surface in exactly the same way as drawing or painting on paper. You describe the image positively, and the marks you make hold the ink for printing.

Monochrome lithographs are comparable in tone and texture to crayon or ink line-and-wash drawings. Colour lithography involves preparing an individual plate for each colour to be printed, but you can build up beautifully wide-ranging effects of surface texture and colour by overprinting.

The lithography process depends on a simple chemical principle – the mutual antipathy of grease and water. The image is drawn with greasy materials on a grease-sensitive surface, with the non-printing areas treated with water-based materials to keep them clean. When printing ink is rolled on, it adheres only to the sensitised, greasy marks. The inked image can be printed on paper either by direct contact or by offsetting; that is, taking up the ink from the plate onto an intermediary surface and laying it down separately on the paper.

Although lithography is such an expressive, painterly medium, the chemical processing can initially seem tedious and difficult to grasp. However, it is carried out in simple stages, all designed to 'set' the image on the lithographic plate.

Tools and materials

Originally, lithographic images were prepared on large blocks of limestone and printed by direct contact. This method is still practised, but it is now more common to use metal plates – zinc or aluminium, depending on which is more easily available. Metal plates can also be printed direct, but are particularly adapted to offset printing. The stone or plate has an even grain which contributes to the characteristic textures of lithographic printing. After printing the surface can be cleaned and resensitised to be used again, but after a few uses it must be completely regrained.

There are specialist services that do this.

For drawing up the image, you can use litho crayons and pencils, and lithographic ink (tusche), brushed on full-strength or as diluted washes. All these materials are black, but once you have drawn and processed the plate, the image can be inked up in any colour for printing.

The plate is treated with a number of chemicals in the processing stages. The undrawn plate is first sensitised with a liquid preparation known as 'counter-etch'. Gum arabic is used to protect non-printing areas while you draw on the plate or to seal the plate surface between stages of processing and printing. The image is 'fixed' on the plate by applying a caustic etch solution, such as a dilute acid mixed with gum. The term 'etch' is confusing if you are already familiar with the physical process of etching on metal – in lithography the etch solution does not eat into the plate surface; it simply helps to set the greasy marks.

At all stages of processing and printing the plate is frequently dampened and dried off. Sponges are common equipment for lithography, and a hairdryer or fan is essential for drying stages – unless you are prepared to wait hours, or even days, before moving on to the next step.

Lithography is a studio-based process, so if you attend a class or work in a commercial studio under supervision, you will find most of what you need already available; ask the tutor or technician whether you are expected to supply any of the materials yourself.

See also
Etching,
pages 84–101

Etching equipment

1 Lithographic stick ink;
2 lithographic crayons;
3 pencil and graphite sticks; **4** lithographic drawing ink; **5** printing ink; **6** large inking roller; **7** zinc litho plate; **8** expandable sponge.

Test plate

Many studios keep printed test sheets that demonstrate the various textures you can obtain by using a range of techniques to draw on the plate with lithographic ink and crayon. Other studio materials can also be used that leave a greasy residue on the plate. The examples shown here are:

1 crayon lines
2 pen and ink lines
3 crayon dragged on its side on a textured surface
4 a solid wash of undiluted litho ink
5 lithographic pencil lines
6 wax pencil lines
7 a wash made with ink floated in water and turpentine
8 tap-water ink wash
9 gum arabic resist under oil-based tusche
10 turpentine wash drawn into with ink
11 sponged ink
12 spattered ink
13 car spray paint

Preparing the plate

There are a few minor variations possible in the steps and materials applied to preparing and processing a lithographic plate. The demonstration shown here describes a standard series of stages, which explains the basic principles and practice, but you may be taught a slightly different method at the studio you work in.

Once the plate surfaces have been prepared, the artist draws and paints on as many plates as necessary for the number of colours to print. A working drawing helps you to identify which details to include on the plate for each colour. To lay out your guidelines you can sketch with charcoal or chalk directly on the plate, or trace down over a chalky transfer paper. The plate is sensitive to any greasy materials (even fingerprints), so do not use pencils or crayons for guidelines not intended to appear in the final print.

For those areas that will appear in the print, you can apply the full range of drawing and painting techniques – for example, line drawing with crayon, brush or pen, free liquid washes, and sponged, spattered and drybrushed textures. It is also possible to make erasures at this stage to correct any errors. When the plate is fully drawn up, the image is dried, dusted and fixed; then it is covered with a layer of gum and must be left, preferably overnight, before the next stage.

Sensitising the plate
1 Hold the plate under running water and allow the whole surface to become fully wet. Drain off the excess water but keep the plate damp.

2 Pour on the counter-etch solution and use a sponge to spread it evenly over the whole surface of the plate.

3 Hold the plate under running water and rinse off the solution thoroughly. Drain off the excess water.

3 Dry off the surface of the plate completely. A hairdryer is a valuable piece of studio equipment, as the need to dry the plate quickly recurs throughout the lithographic process.

4 Sponge gum arabic around the edges of the plate to make a border for the image area. Allow the gum to dry.

Working study
The lithograph shown in the following demonstration is to print in only two colours, so the artist has prepared her idea of the image quite carefully beforehand in a sketch and more detailed colour study (above). This gives her guidelines for the basic shapes in the composition,
the balance of tones and the interaction of line work with broader areas of colour. However, as the image is allowed to develop freely as the plates are prepared, the finished lithograph (see page 123) will be different in character and detail.

Drawing on the plate

1 To transfer the guidelines of a working drawing to the plate you must use a non-greasy transfer paper so the lines will not appear after processing of the image.

2 Place your drawing over the transfer paper and work over it with a pencil or pen to press the main lines of the image down onto the plate.

3 Start to draw direct on the plate with a lithographic crayon or pencil. You can work exactly as you would with chalk or pencil on paper.

6 Continue until the image is completed in as much detail as you require. Keep in mind that this image will print uniformly as tones of one colour.

4 Apply the lithographic ink with paintbrushes, again working as you would on paper. You can use the ink at full strength or diluted with distilled or tap water.

5 You can apply ink with a sponge, as here, or with a rag or other applicator to vary the textures of your drawing. Here, paper masks are used to contain the sponging.

First-stage processing
1 When all the ink drawing is completely dry, dust over the plate with French chalk, spread with clean cotton wool or a soft cloth.

3 Brush on the liquid-etch solution, covering the whole surface of the plate evenly and generously. This helps to 'fix' the drawn image on the plate. Leave it on for just a couple of minutes.

4 Put the plate under running water and rinse off the etch solution thoroughly. Use the hairdryer to dry off the plate completely.

2 Repeat the dusting process with powdered resin. These dry materials temporarily counteract the greasiness in the image, so it will accept liquid processing in the next stage.

5 Sponge a thin layer of gum arabic over the whole plate surface and allow it to dry. Leave the plate overnight before continuing the processing.

Processing the image

This stage is a second 'etch' that strengthens the effect of the greasy marks on the plate surface. It is very similar to the preparatory stages, except that this time the drawn image is washed out and the marks are treated with asphaltum or printing ink. This makes the colour appear different, but as you take out the original drawing and put colour back in you have the opportunity to check how effectively the marks have set into the grain of the plate. This is where you begin to see the real appearance of the image for print and can judge how well the textures have developed. Again there is an opportunity for correction, using an erasing fluid.

When the image is satisfactory, it is rolled up with ink as if for printing, gummed and left to stand. The processing stages are repetitive, but as with any technical methods you will soon become quicker and more expert in seeing them through.

Second-stage processing
1 Use white spirit and a clean rag to wash out the drawn image from the surface of the plate. All the black disappears, but you can still see the marks as a greasy 'shadow' on the plate. The gum is unaffected by white spirit and continues to protect undrawn areas of the plate.

2 Rub in a thin layer of printing ink. This helps to reinforce the image and preserves delicate wash effects. Alternatively, you can use asphaltum, which strengthens the textures and is better suited to a heavier, more dense drawing.

3 Wipe out the ink with white spirit, then wash off the plate with water to remove the gummed layer still surrounding the image.

4 Roll up the damp plate with printing ink. The image now appears as it will print. Dry off the plate and cover the surface with gum. Let it stand for at least half an hour.

Printing

This sequence demonstrates offset printing in two colours from metal plates. The basic techniques are the same for direct printing from stone or metal, except for the action of the press.

Generally, a litho plate is inked with a large, wide roller that covers the width of the image area in one pass, giving an even, consistent coverage of colour. The difference between lithography and the other processes as far as printing is concerned is that the plate has to be wetted before any ink is applied and kept damp while it is rolled up. The water protects the clean, non-printing areas of the plate but does not affect the ink's adherence to the greasy printing areas.

When the ink layer is dense and even enough to print, the plate must be dried off completely before paper and plate are positioned on the bed of the press. The mechanism of the press brings the thick rubber 'blanket' of the roller into contact with the plate on the first pass, and on the way back the roller is pressed over the paper, transferring the inked image. It may take two or three passes to build up sufficient ink on the roller to print off clearly. You can then run your final prints.

When printing in two or more colours, the basic procedure for each one is the same, but you need to register them accurately on the previous printing. There are various ways of registering, but most presses are equipped with grippers and stops that enable you to position the paper correctly in relation to each plate. In this example, the second colour is first printed on an acetate sheet attached to one end of the press. The print of the first colour is positioned underneath the acetate, aligning the colour areas. The stops are then set to the edges of the printing paper so that further prints can be slipped into place.

Offset printing
1 Mix up a quantity of printing ink and roll it out evenly on a glass slab. Use a large roller that will cover the image area. The artist is working here with a gradated tone of pink; she has mixed three tones of the same colour and rolled them out together.

2 Use a wet sponge to remove the gum arabic from the plate. Position the plate on the bed of the offset press. Keep it damp throughout the rolling-up process.

3 Roll the colour over the image area on the plate firmly and evenly. As necessary, wipe the surface with a damp sponge to remove any ink residue that may float on the non-printing surface.

4 When a sufficiently heavy and even colour layer has adhered to the image, dry off the plate completely. If it remains damp, moisture will be picked up on the press roller and spread onto the printing paper.

5 Roll the press roller back and forth over the inked plate until the image is clearly picked up on the roller 'blanket' (the rubber covering). Mechanisms for these presses vary; at this stage the roller is not making contact with the area where the paper lies on the press bed.

6 Position the paper on the bed of the press adjacent to the plate. The press has grippers to keep the paper flat and in place. Take the roller over the plate and back to pass over and make contact with the paper, laying down the inked image.

7 In the first printing, the main shapes are all in place within the image but the tones and textures are very delicate. The artist has to visualise how the imposition of a second colour will add the depth and detail needed to sharpen and complete the rendering.

Registering the second colour

1 The artist has planned this print so that both colours are gradated, giving tonal variation across the whole image. She lays out the three mixed tones of the second colour on the mixing slab.

3 The plate is put in place on the press and inked with blue. The first print is taken, by the same technique as previously, on a sheet of acetate anchored at one end of the press.

2 The large roller is used to work the ink evenly back and forth on the glass slab, until the three colours merge together smoothly.

4 A print from the first plate is positioned under the acetate and moved until the image areas register exactly.

5 Keeping the print in place, the artist adjusts the stops on the press that butt to the side and bottom edges of the printing paper. Methods of registering and marking the position of the paper may vary, depending on the press model.

6 The second colour is printed onto each of the pink prints, each time positioning the paper against the fixed stops and holding it in place with the grippers. As before, the roller is taken across the press over the plate, then back to lay down the blue image on the print.

7 In the final print, the strength of the blue tones emphasises particular shapes, as does the greater amount of linear drawing included in this image. But the two colours integrate convincingly to give the still life depth and form.

Themes

Learning to use a printmaking medium creatively is a two-stage process. First you have to find out what it does; then you have to see how that potential applies to the style and content of your work. One way to learn is by looking at finished prints and understanding how they have been constructed, and the inventive ways in which the artists have exploited these processes. This gallery section exhibits a variety of media, subject matter and styles of work, as much as possible related directly to the techniques already described.

Line and tone

- MONOCHROME PRINTS
- LINE QUALITIES
- SHADING AND LAYERING

▲ **CAROLE KATCHEN**
EMBROIDERED HAT (MONOPRINT)
The printed impression reflects the spontaneity of vigorous brush-drawn lines in this rendering. Their boldness is enhanced by the transition through subtle colour variations that describe different parts of the figure. Open, irregular shapes created by the outline drawing are offset by the repetitive detail of the patterned areas.

Line is a particularly strong element of relief prints and certain intaglio processes, because of the basic techniques in these media and the physical character of the materials used. In monochrome linocuts and woodcuts, where lines form the boundaries of shapes and contribute pattern and detail to the rendering, line qualities are often relied upon to develop visual interest. The quality can vary according to the texture of the relief block – fine line work can be difficult on coarse-grained wood, for example. Such practical considerations need to be accommodated when you consider a style of work suited to the subject.

Drypoint is essentially a linear medium, and etching is said to have the most expressive and variable line qualities of all print media, because these derive from both your drawing skills and the action of the acid. However, you rarely see an etching that is completed in line only – more often the line work is combined with smooth aquatint tones and coarser textures created in a variety of ways.

All of these media also lend themselves to black-and-white renderings, from the strong graphic contrast of relief prints to the subtle shadings of aquatint. Since it is always technically possible to include colour, a strictly monochromatic interpretation is the artist's deliberate choice. It can contribute a pleasing simplicity and directness, or a complex, layered and textured effect, like a heavily worked drawing.

Monoprint and lithography are more painterly media, inviting you to exploit the effects of broad areas of tone and colour. Pure line drawing is unusual in a monoprint, and it has to be done with a 'broad brush' approach, but the example on this page shows how vigorous and colourful it can be, despite the economy of means. In lithography, the balance of line with mass and texture in a composition is largely a matter of the individual artist's style and the special features of the subject – all kinds of effects associated with crayon or pen drawing and watercolour painting can be achieved, using a limited palette or full colour range. Glorious colour is one of the great pleasures of screenprinting, but this does not preclude the use of linear elements; and tonal balance is an important ingredient of making strong colours work effectively.

▲ **VANESSA LUBACH**
MOUSEHOLE WINDOWSILL (LINOCUT)

The variation and intricacy of line work in this linocut builds texture and detail to reflect a moment of crisp stillness at Mousehole Harbour on a summer's night. Eight separate colour layers were used, from pale creams to rich blues, under a detailed, dark blue final layer. This was a challenging project for the artist, and several recarvings were necessary. The linocut is part of an ongoing theme of windowsill views, drawing on the concept of a landscape viewed through the frame of domesticity.

St Pancras Station 5/6 June, 1983   Caroline Bilson

◄ **CAROLINE BILSON**
ST PANCRAS STATION
(LITHOGRAPH)

This print creates such a finely varied impression of the architectural detail in the subject, it is surprising to discover that the line work is drawn freely and decisively with the relatively coarse medium of lithographic crayon. To give full impact to the intricate structure, the colour is confined to gentle washes of diluted litho ink, using evenly matched mid-tones of warm red and neutral grey. More emphatic tonal variation occurs where the washes are combined with roughly shaded crayon textures.

▶ **CELIA LEWIS**
BARN OWL
(LINOCUT)

Having experimented with repeating the background print using a small piece of lino that would be put through the press several times, the artist decided to repeat the pattern on a single sheet of lino instead. The area where the owl would be was masked out and the plate then put through the press. There is a vibrancy and variety of line quality wherever you cast your eye over this linocut.

7/50   Spring Washing.   Louise Grace

◀ **PAMELA GRACE**
SPRING WASHING
(LITHOGRAPH)
The underlying drawing was
designed to reveal the structure of
the trees before the leaves came
out. The restrained palette
contrasts with the splashes of
colour of the family washing,
draped between the trees, while
the layers of foliage in the
foreground represent the slow
transition from winter to spring.

▶ **TANIA BEAUMONT**
SHORELINE (LINOCUT)
This print is part of a series of
works completed after a trip to the
beaches of southwest Ireland. The
foreground images of seaweed and
solid stones were cut from lino,
while the main pebble background
was cut from a rubber shower mat
found on the side of the street,
which attracted the artist because
of its interesting texture.

Graphic impact

■ LINE AND SHAPE ■ EDGE QUALITIES

■ CONTRAST

▲ **IAN SCOTT MASSIE**
RIBBLEHEAD BLUE (SCREENPRINT)
The design for this print draws heavily on the iconography of early transport posters. The perspective, dynamic movement and strong colour taken from a limited palette all contribute to the impact of the image.

A picture that has strong graphic impact draws your attention immediately. There are certain elements of style and composition that practically guarantee this kind of instant attraction – calligraphic line, bold shapes, hard edges, powerful tonal contrast, bright colour, repetitive pattern. All these are used to draw the eye to ephemeral graphic communications, such as posters and advertisements. The pitfall for the artist is that relying on these elements too simplistically can create an image that has impact but reveals all in the first viewing. Ideally, a fine art print is something that can stand long or close acquaintance, so the initial impression contains additional subtleties to be discovered and appreciated.

What usually delivers this more lasting richness is a degree of variability, an unexpected touch. The relief-printing media, especially woodcut and linocut, lend themselves to apparently simple, impactful approaches – clear-cut, black-and-white images are typical of these processes, and naturally make strong graphics. They need to contain beautiful or disturbing shapes; controlled but fluid line work; distinct edge qualities; crackling textures. Making use of a medium's restrictions can sometimes be as effective as trying to extend its potential – for example, the strictly practical advantages of monochrome block prints are that they are easy to produce and the materials are inexpensive.

The techniques of preparing and printing lithographs, screenprints and etchings invite you to conceive images with a more complex amount of layering or surface activity. Of these media, screenprinting is most likely to be associated with strikingly graphic imagery; certain stencil processes encourage this quality, and the process has been widely used for printing posters. Lithography, too, has a direct association with posters and illustrations; its graphic qualities can combine with or supersede its more painterly effects. Pictorial impact can come from dynamic composition or vibrant colour.

Etching is characteristically a more reticent and subtle medium, but because you can apply many different techniques to a single plate, all etchings have an underlying graphic unity that draws together the variations of line, tone, texture and colour. This makes an etched image all the more expressive, whether simple or complex.

▶ **CELIA LEWIS**
MIXED TULIPS (LINOCUT)
The instant graphic impact of the solidly coloured tulips and their stems and leaves is 'framed' by the more intricate patterning on the vase. The bright flowers and monochrome vase play off each other and invite further study as the eye travels between blooms and vase.

▶ LIZ MYHILL
TIDELINE ODDMENTS (LINOCUT)

In this piece the artist has created a series of pleasing shapes that form a bold design, and used a limited palette of related colours for a calm mood. The print reflects memories of a fishing village location, combining found objects with their landscape context. The artist prefers to keep sketches to a minimum, which gives her the freedom to enjoy the sinuous lines and marks achieved by a gouge, without the temptation to attempt replicating a sketch.

18/22   Tideline Oddments   Liz Myhill 08

▶ ANITA REYNOLDS
ESCAPING THE SWALE (MONOPRINT AND DRYPOINT)

The annual burning of the gorse (swale) on Dartmoor provided the starting point for this print. The first layer is a colour monoprint using torn paper stencils that create the impression of flames licking their way up and off the print. The second, drypoint, layer provides the stark contrast between the silent yet destructive flames and the noisy, escaping crows. The image is one of panic and excitement with an underlying beauty. The birds punctuating the upper section of the print create dynamic negative spaces.

▲ JONATHAN HEALE
CATNAPS EDITION
(WOODCUT)

A simple, everyday subject becomes an unusual, witty composition when seen from an unexpected angle. By treating the human subject almost as a background element, the artist uses a strong combination of large and small shapes, and makes the most of the bright patterning that frames the simple, elegant form of the cat. The print is a black-and-white woodcut hand-coloured with watercolour paint.

◀ VANESSA LUBACH
FAREWELL TO A NORFOLK
SUMMER (LINOCUT)

This multilayer linocut depicts the backlighting of a clump of trees in autumn, when the light coming through the overlapping branches makes the trees look like feathers. The overprinting of multiple colours gives a great richness of tones, especially since the yellow underlies every subsequent layer. The final, intricately carved key block gives texture and rhythm to the composition.

▼ HELEN PEYTON
PHILIPS SILVERWING (LINOCUT)

Made out of rubber and very much of their time, these Edwardian swimming shoes inspired love and admiration in all that saw them at the artist's pop-up museum. This affection has been represented using the graphic qualities of block printing, a purity of colour and a cleanness of line to enhance the historical nature of the subject.

Pattern and texture

- SURFACE VALUES
- VARYING TONE AND TEXTURE
- FORMAL PATTERNS

Many prints are executed in black and white or a restricted colour range, which in turn restricts your use of colour as a way of varying the surface qualities and making the shapes interactive. Certain media, particularly block prints, also preclude the subtleties of shading conventionally used to model form. Pattern and texture can perform both of these functions in a composition, so they are particularly important elements of printmaking.

Texture works in three distinct ways in prints; firstly, each medium has characteristic textural qualities to do with the materials and the kinds of marks that you can make on or with them – one of the most easily identifiable examples is the slight graininess typical of lithographs, because the litho plate itself has a definite grain; there is a similar effect in the aquatint process in etching. You can also use different techniques to create textures intended to match or stand in for specific textures in the subject; or you can exploit similar processes simply to make the surface of the print more interesting.

Pattern is not inherent in printmaking materials, but in some cases the patterns you can easily make are directly related to the tools. The V-tools and gouges used in linocut and woodcut lend themselves to broadly hatched lines – straight, curving or spiralled – and relatively coarse dot patterns or V-shaped, short cuts. A drypoint or etching needle is ideal for fine hatching and crosshatching, and also delicate stippling. Wood-engraving tools have a lighter touch than gouges, but cut more broadly than intaglio needles. Discreet patterns of lines and dots are a way of creating shading and gentle gradations of tone, and have been used as such in prints and drawings for centuries.

There is a crossover between pattern and texture in purely visual terms. The texture of foliage, for example, might be simulated by making a rough pattern of aquatint tones. Sometimes it is the overall feeling for shape and structure in the image that creates an impression of patterning, whether or not individual shapes contain surface variation.

◀ **ELISABETH HARDEN**
GOLDFISH (LITHOGRAPH)

The translucency and reflectiveness of the goldfish pool are conveyed by preparing the plate images with lightweight crayon drawing and washes of lithographic ink, then printing with semi-transparent layers of colour. The cool, neutral colour range works equally effectively in representing the water and the stone statue. Broad shading in warm yellow suggests the denser textures of flowers and foliage.

▶ **LYNNE ROEBUCK**
BEDTIME STORIES (LINOCUT)

Texture and pattern in this print of Whitby Harbour successfully suggest movement, land surface quality and light. Texture has been created by cutting the lino block in different ways, as well as by alternately rolling ink in a light 'dry' state or thickly. The reddish-brown has a very subtle mottling and unevenness, which suggests soft granular soil, while the black is dense, opaque and smooth.

▶ DAVID KOSTER
BURNET MOTH (LITHOGRAPH)
There is a strong linear quality to
this composition which creates
both visual texture within the print
and a sense of the natural textures
in the subject. The artist draws in
litho ink, using quill pens and
brushes, to prepare the black
plate, which forms the key design
for additional colour plates. The
inks are made very transparent,
to gain the maximum effect from
overprinting. This also emphasises
the grain and fragile edge qualities
of the washes. Occasionally, the
artist adds touches of strong
colour by direct stencilling onto
the finished print, where a small
colour area does not justify
processing of another plate.

▲ **RICHARD DON GABRIEL**
BATHING WOMEN (WOODCUT)
This image captures a lively sense of movement and interaction by concentrating each element of the subject into a formal pattern device. The balance of tones is beautifully organised by letting the white play a strong role in the mosaic and striped patterns that represent the swirling water, while keeping the patterns of the women's clothing relatively dark so that their bodies form graceful black silhouettes. On a close-grained wood block the cut shapes remain crisp and the ink prints with an even, dense texture.

▼ PHIL GREENWOOD
MEADOW CLOCKS (ETCHING)
In painting, the colour interest of a landscape subject often dominates, drawing attention to the broad impression rather than the intricate detail. But the natural textures of grass, foliage and flowers are ideal for the scale and subtlety of etching. The complex tracery of linear drawing in the foreground is sharpened by the soft aquatint texture of the dark trees, and this textural balance is further developed by the strong tonal pattern of the image.

▲ PAUL BARTLETT
THE EMPTY CHAIR (ETCHING)
The sugar-lift etching technique enabled the artist to make a detailed painting of the subject on zinc plate and reproduce the shapes positively. The plate was coated with aquatint resin, so the image would etch with subtle tonal variations and a grainy texture. A striking, almost photographic, effect is achieved through the well-judged combination of meticulous, small-scale detail and boldly contrasted, broad areas of light and shadow.

◀ LORALIE CLEMMENSEN
BROOMS, KYOTO (LINOCUT)
The rough texture of the brooms and smooth look of their bamboo handles is well executed in this linocut print. The pattern of the hanging brooms is important compositionally, as is the shadow area behind and under them. A single linoleum plate is used in this reduction technique. The colour and tonal quality of each new layer is affected by the previous layers. Unexpected challenges continually arise until the print declares itself finished.

◄ MARY GILLETT
ASCENT (ETCHING)

After corroding a tracery of fine marks drawn into a hard ground, the sugar-lift technique was applied using a random mark-making process that exploited the effects of water and oil as they resisted each other. The plate was bitten using the open-bite method and the sugar-lift technique was repeated with the addition of an aquatint ground, so as to allow tonal variations and create further textures and patterns across the plate. This subtle layering of techniques was combined with modifications made by the judicious use of the burnishing and scraping tool. Characterised by the looseness of this mark-making process and capitalising on some accidental corrosion of the plate, the image conveys atmosphere and depth without the trappings of irrelevant detail.

◄ KIT BOYD
THE BLUE NEO-ROMANTIC (ETCHING)

This print began as a detailed etching, followed by an aquatint for the shading. The detailed marks made by the etching needle to create tone on the grassy banks and the patterned bark of the trees, with tiny dots and variations in mark to create tones through pattern, can be seen in areas underneath and untouched by the aquatint. The aquatint's graded tone in the sky was created by gently lifting and lowering the plate at an angle in the acid bath, so that the top of the plate was bitten more and therefore printed darker than the horizon line.

◄ REBECCA OWENS
JAPANESE FISH
(MONOPRINT AND LINOCUT)

This print successfully integrates a limited selection of strong colours, using pattern to enliven the stylised, simplified shapes. Broad colour areas were put on paper by monoprinting, then the cut lino block was printed over them in red and dark green, using small rollers or a brush to apply the different colours to the block. The darker red in the fishes' patterning was applied by hand after printing.

Colour

- ADDING COLOUR
- THE PRINTMAKER'S PALETTE
- DESCRIPTIVE AND EXPRESSIVE COLOUR

Colour plays a variety of roles in printmaking, one of which is to add a purely decorative element to images that were planned to work successfully in black and white. Two simple ways of imposing colour on a monochromatic design are hand-colouring with watercolour or gouache, or applying collage to the paper before or after printing. You maintain the advantage of being able to produce multiple, identical prints, but combined with the means of making each one an individual interpretation.

More frequently, colour is not just decorative but descriptive, relating directly to the colours of the subject; or expressive, conveying something about the artist's response to the subject and sometimes forming a characteristic element of personal style. Most of the printmaking media can easily accommodate multi-coloured images – any restriction is imposed not by the materials available, but by the effort you want to put into developing the image. Screen-printing, for example, has a potentially infinite colour range – you can pre-mix as on the painter's palette. But to combine many colours, even when mixtures are produced by overprinting, you have to repeat many times the physical labour of preparing stencils, pulling prints, registering colours and cleaning down the screen mesh.

It can be difficult to plan many successive colour layers, and the graphic qualities of a print may be lost if the colour relationships are too complex and busy. You need the confidence to predict how the colour combinations will appear after all the printing stages, and perhaps to adjust your expectations during processing. A limited palette is often the wisest choice because it is a controlled form of expression. Some artists enjoy printmaking precisely for this reason – they find working as imaginatively as possible with well-defined processing stages more sympathetic than the apparent freedom of direct painting techniques, which can leave the questions of how to start and when to stop too bewilderingly open-ended.

Colour in intaglio printing is often more limited, muted and subtle than in other media because of the inking and printing methods. Bright or strong hues may be introduced as local colour or to create a mood, while line and tone form the structure of the image. There is typically more emphasis on tonality than on colourfulness, but the effects can be very richly textured.

◀ **LIZ MYHILL**
FOX II (LINOCUT)

This piece is based on the precious moments when wildlife can be observed without disturbing it. The red fox and setting sun really stand out against the strictly limited monochrome palette, with the half-tone in the fields adding texture and interest. The artist likes to break up the shapes that define the edge of a print. The bullrushes draw us into the picture, but also screen us from the fox, reinforcing the idea that we have caught it unawares and absorbed in the movement of the birds whirling overhead.

▲ **PIP CARPENTER**
THREE POMEGRANATES (ETCHING)
A rich, descriptive colour effect has been achieved by printing from two plates – one inked in blue, the other with gradations of crimson, red, orange and yellow. In the lower part of the picture the blue lines and aquatinting provide local colour and tone; in the fruits and background, blue creates a dark undertone for the warm colours.

◄ **IAN SCOTT MASSIE**
EDINBURGH MORNING (SCREENPRINT)
The limited colour palette of this screenprint advances in stronger and stronger tones. The limited palette unifies the image while the varying tones give depth. This is a reduction print and therefore successive layers are registered over each other to intensify the tonal qualities of the print.

▲ **MANDY PAYNE**
LIMINAL ZONE (MONOPRINT AND COLLAGE)
The artist uses a biro to draw onto thin paper placed on a lightly inked slab. The resulting image is reversed and picks up multiple, random, smudgy marks from the inked slab surface as well as the stronger drawn line. The collaged red lamp-post and white railings add vibrancy and contrast.

▶ **PIP CARPENTER**
HYACINTHS (DRYPOINT)
A subject which has a strong pattern of individual shapes as well as integral vivid hues can be equally effective interpreted in monochrome or colour. The potential for hand-colouring black-and-white prints leaves the artist free to make choices about the final presentation. Here the sensitive lines and rich blacks of the drypoint drawing are enhanced by vibrant watercolour washes built to varying strengths.

◀ **JUNE ANN SULLIVAN**
BEACH PEOPLE (MONOPRINT)
The image is prepared for printing using etching inks, with solvent to vary the textures. Where the ink is thickest, the colours are vivid and rich; together with the broad white highlights where the paper is left bare, this creates the sunny mood of the picture. The foreground was added using a transparent ink base with a touch of colour.

▲ **REBECCA OWENS**
SUMMER FRUITS
(MONOPRINT AND LINOCUT)

This lush, naturalistic colour rendering was built up
in three layers. Background colour and undertones
were first applied as a monoprint. The cut lino block
describing the shapes and textures of the fruits was
then inked in several colours, using small rollers and
brushes to apply water-based block-printing inks, and
overprinted on the first colour layer. Small touches
intended to bring out the textural detail were added by
hand, such as the opaque white highlights that put the
final gloss on the cherries.

◄ **PAMELA GRACE**
SEPTEMBER, STOKESLEY
(LITHOGRAPH)

This lithograph is based on detailed
pencil drawings, and uses three colour
plates. The washed-back greens and
blues convey the subtle effects of the
vegetables, with the cream tone of the
paper providing plenty of space and
light between them and ensuring that
the colours remain distinct. The pink
and orange tones are painted by hand.

▲ **KIT BOYD**
READING DARK MOUNTAIN
(ETCHING)

The warm, olive-green ink chosen for
this monochrome etching creates a
feeling of bucolic calm and safety, the
tones of the aquatint adding to the
gentleness of the pastoral scene. If it
had been printed simply in black, the
soft light of the day would appear
harsher, and the mood of the piece
would be altered entirely.

◀ IAN MOWFORTH
MACKEREL (LINOCUT)
The simple, graphic shape and patterning of the fish are provided by the lino block. The glittering colours of the fish skin come from a collage of various materials, including silver leaf, coloured tissues and printed papers. These were assembled on thin textured paper, which was then laid over the inked block to print the linocut. Because the paper is translucent, it was possible to see through it clearly to register the collage correctly over the black line work on the block.

▶ SALLY ROBSON
ROYAL HILL, GREENWICH (ETCHING)
Even when an image is mainly dependent on effects of line and tone for its descriptive qualities, colour printing can add both visual interest and touches of local colour. In this attractively 'stacked' composition depicting closely built streets full of architectural detail, the subtle, warm colours create a more inviting mood than hard black, without detracting from the intricacy of the graphic interpretation.

▶ CELIA LEWIS
PUFFIN II (LINOCUT)
The artist often puts three or four colours on the inking plate and rolls the ink on in one go with one roller – touching up with a smaller roller where necessary. To print the background, the puffin shape was masked out, and then carefully dropped into place later. The aqua green-blue background colour perfectly complements the depiction of this coastal, cliff-dwelling bird.

Composition

- FRAMING THE IMAGE
- BALANCE AND RHYTHM
- DIVIDING THE PICTURE PLANE

A printed image frequently requires more careful preliminary organisation than a drawing or painting that can evolve freely on the working surface. The composition must relate effectively to the scale and proportions of the base material on which the image is prepared – particularly on a block or plate because its edges usually show in the print. If part of the image is put down in the wrong place, or is out of proportion, it can be difficult to amend or erase it. If you are printing in more than one colour, you need to be able to locate the colours accurately in separate printings, to register finally as a unified image.

You cannot tell exactly what you will see in a finished print until you print it, so many artists like to get a firm sense of composition through a working drawing or colour study before beginning to work within the print process. The initial study may be used only as a reference guide, or can be traced off to form the basis of the print.

The elements of composition in printmaking are no different from those in any other artists' medium. The overall picture needs some kind of rhythm or balance – this can be mainly created by lines or by solid shapes and masses, with stresses running vertically and horizontally across the picture plane, diagonally or randomly. The image can be centralised and contained, or strongly related to the edges of the outer 'frame'. The shapes can be presented flatly, modelled with colour and tone, or activated with patterns and textures. The spatial arrangement may be descriptive or formalised, recreating what is seen in the subject or interpreting your impression.

The variety of options you have depends both on the medium you are working in and the nature of your subject. None of the print-making processes imposes absolute restrictions on the form of a composition, but you need to consider the character of your medium as you plan the image – the means of creating texture are, for example, less complex and subtle in linocut than in lithography. The pictures in this section are chosen to show how artists work inventively within the disciplines of their media, as well as demonstrating particular forms of pictorial organisation.

◀ **THERESA PATEMAN**
SPIKE OF THE OLD KENT ROAD (LINOCUT)
This witty linocut emphasises the character of the dog by making him a massive, self-contained presence occupying more than half of the picture area. This creates a very clean, strong division between the black and white shapes, although the strong linear detail conveys a sense of movement and interaction between different parts of the image.

◀ **HELEN PEYTON**
BOBBIN (LINOCUT)

Designed to represent the layout in a museum's collections case, this piece was deliberately drawn to reflect a reverence for the subject by giving each bobbin its own space and showcasing the different thread colours. The 26-colour reduction took over six weeks to complete, from drawings to finished linocut. The artist spends a considerable time on artist proofs, working out different colourways or further cutting.

▶ **GLYNN THOMAS**
PIN MILL WINDOW (ETCHING)
A frame within a frame is an interesting way of dividing the picture surface formally. In this case, the window panes create a very balanced, regular division, but the view beyond the window fills each rectangle actively in a different way. The informal, curving and diagonal lines of the boats' riggings play against the fixed horizontal and vertical framing.

▲ **SUSIE PERRING**
TRICK CYCLIST (ETCHING)
The spotlit 'cyclist' is the centre of attention in the physical centre of the rectangle on which he is drawn. The shapes are simplified, but beautifully suggestive of mood and atmosphere, with active textures in the black areas that modify the harshness of such a strong tonal contrast. The rich, velvety marks were formed by impressing a soft etching ground.

◀ LYNNE ROEBUCK
COAST (LINOCUT)

This seemingly simple print required a great deak of attention during the working drawing stage. The artist explored using different proportions of sea to land, land and sea shapes, and ways of breaking these shapes down further. The print is dominated by horizontal lines, interrupted by the vertical cliffs. Given the horizontal lines have a subtly different style, it's satisfying rather than crude. Dominance is a powerful device in composition – the effect here is that the eye is drawn to the cliffs and then on to the distant headland.

▲ LINDA RICHARDSON
MARCH HARES (LINOCUT)

This print was created from three lino blocks, with one block cut twice, making it in part a reduction cut. The constraints of cutting lino encourage the artist to work with pattern, shape and blocks of colour. Transparent inks give the feeling of distance in the background.

▲ **COLIN SEE-PAYNTON**
PUFFINS (WOOD ENGRAVING)
The hard end-grain blocks used in wood engraving enable the artist to control fine cutting techniques that create intricate texture. The halftone effect of stippling and hatching is beautifully balanced with solid areas of black and white. Every shape contributes to the rhythmic flow of the composition, which is both accentuated and counterpointed by the changing emphasis of the rippling lines.

1/50   Katch 1980

▲ **CAROLE KATCHEN**
YORUBA MAN (ETCHING)
The figure makes a beautiful, fluid shape placed boldly at the centre of the image area. An overly symmetrical sense of balance is avoided by the slant of his relaxed posture and the off-centre shape of the table leading out of the frame in the foreground, which together produce a diagonal pull through the image. The contrast of tonal shading and plain against patterned areas is perfectly judged.

▲ **HELEN MURGATROYD**
SIMMER LENTILS UNTIL JUST TENDER (LINOCUT)
This linocut is part of a series of six prints illustrating each stage in a lentil salad recipe. Variations in tone and a suggestion of depth are achieved using different weights of line and dots.

◀ **PETER STRACHAN**
NORMANDY BEACH (SCREENPRINT)
The sky is often a significant feature of an outdoor view, but a very bold decision has been made here in allowing it to dominate the picture so dramatically. The intensity of the heavy, flat blue is offset by the vivid handling of light striking the white buildings on the beach. This artist typically uses hand-painted and sometimes cut-paper stencils combined with photographic imagery. Special facilities are required to prepare photo-stencils and expose them on the screen; photo techniques can also be applied to etching and litho plates.

▼ **JO AUSTEN**
YOU LEFT WITHOUT SAYING GOODBYE (ETCHING)
In this print, conventional perspective is used in combination with an enlarged scale in the foreground, inviting the viewer to share in the depicted stag beetle's perspective, and adding a sense of the surreal. The sprawling trees and flowers are cut off by the frame, suggesting there is more going on in this semi-magical scene than meets the eye.

▲ **HELEN MURGATROYD**
DAL BHAT DINNER (LINOCUT)
This single-colour linocut captures a typical Nepali dinner scene. By cutting and collaging her observational drawings, Helen Murgatroyd carefully maps out her composition before carving the lino. Other decisions about light, tone and pattern are made during the carving process, with several proof prints taken before the final print is editioned.

Mood and atmosphere

- TONE AND COLOUR
- QUALITIES OF LIGHT
- CREATING SPACE

Certain subjects are attractive because they convey a particular mood or sense of place that becomes an important factor in the artist's interpretation. Often this is best conveyed not by making a literal description of the subject, but by enhancing some quality within it that conveys the impression of mood and atmosphere.

Local colours – the colours that things really are – may be much modified by atmospheric effects or the pattern of light, especially in open landscape or in a shadowy interior. The typically restricted palette of a colour print can be surprisingly effective in rendering these visual sensations. The artist can avoid distracting detail and focus on essential qualities of space, form and light. This may mean organising the variations of colour, tone and texture more rigorously than in a painting, where individual brushstrokes can deal with fleeting and subtle transitions. An image prepared for print must achieve a similar impact by more economical means.

The atmospherics of light are perhaps easiest to handle when there are distinct contrasts of light and shadow, especially in a medium that encourages strong monochromatic interpretation, like etching or wood engraving. Dramatic contrast is interesting, and needs careful management to achieve a coherent image without flattening the drama. Making light and space with colour is a definite challenge, particularly where the image has a fairly balanced, even key in the light or mid-tonal range. Close relationships of hue and tone convey space and mood by subtle interactions – the detail and texture of the image play a significant role. A highly detailed drawing brings the viewer into the subject, whereas dissolving forms and contours open out the pictorial space.

Whatever your medium, the balance of tone and colour is not immediately visible on the plate, block or screen that you are working with. With experience, you learn more about the way the marks you make will translate into print, but the proofing stage is always an exciting moment, when you see your idea take shape. The marks and the colours often remain open to adjustment until the final stages, enabling you to achieve images that are both precisely controlled and highly expressive, like the examples shown here.

◀ **JANE DANIELL**
THAT'S WOUND BY A KEY (ETCHING)

This print has a mysterious, eerie feel and is reminiscent of folklore and fairy tales. The aquatint etching is made using two zinc plates and soft and hard ground. One plate carries the images and the second plate the background of sepia and pink. The tones are achieved by applying aquatint, masking out the light areas before immersing in acid. Areas that are not masked are bitten by the acid to an increasing depth with each immersion. The 'doll's' skirt achieves its texture by impressing scrim into the soft ground. The aquatinting resin is deliberately scattered randomly to achieve the textured background.

◀ JOY BRAND
OLD BREAKWATER
(LITHOGRAPH)

The gentle tones and textures that can be achieved with lithographic painting techniques enable the artist to produce a very delicate and subtle effect of light on water. The rendering is sparing of detail and effectively employs the limited palette to develop the spacious, atmospheric feeling of the view.

▲ KIT BOYD
A RURAL RHAPSODY (ETCHING)

The depth in this etching on copper is created by the line composition of rolling hills and trees, and also through the use of aquatint that has had only a few seconds in acid for the lighter background landscape and five minutes for the stronger tones in the foreground. The highly detailed foreground full of birds and insects focuses the eye, while the dynamic between the two foxes leads the viewer into the hazy distant landscape and beyond.

▲ DONALD HARRIS
FLURRY (ETCHING)
Rich, flat aquatint tones provide an atmospheric background to the whirling pattern of the birds and rippling water. The depth and mood of the image are enhanced by the colour gradations and occasional strong contrasts. Two plates were overprinted to obtain this range, one inked in blues passing from turquoise to violet, the other in yellow, orange and red.

▶ GLYNN THOMAS
KERSEY GARDEN (ETCHING)
The yellow-green predominant in this charming composition gives a sunny, bright tone to the image, with the contrast of brown and dark green contributing space and depth. These colours were all inked together on the plate and printed in one: the brilliant red and yellow touches in the flowers were painted on the cleaned plate and overprinted.

▲ **REBECCA OWENS**
TULIPS 2 (LINOCUT)
Linocut prints made on white tissue paper are collaged together, contrasting the fluid shapes of tulip flowers and leaves with the geometric composition of the collage. The rhythmic patterns in organic forms inspire the artist, who is also interested in the delicacy and semi-transparent nature of thin paper. The overlaying of the bold lino prints creates unexpected focal points and the subtle range of colours is also intriguing.

Style and content

- NARRATIVE
- STYLISTIC INTERPRETATION
- FORMALISED IMAGES

Relief and intaglio printing have a long association with the traditions of graphic communication – woodcuts, for example, were one of the earliest forms of book illustration. These media readily lend themselves to subjects that seem to illustrate a storyline or contain a narrative of their own, in simple, direct images that 'speak' to the viewer. Such subjects can be found in literary sources, in the incidents of everyday life or in special events, representing particular or universal themes. Also in keeping with the narrative element, an artist may produce a series or suite of prints on one theme; the scale and detail of printed images provide suitable means of 'publishing' information, commentary and observation.

Apart from describing related events and images, a series of prints can also be unified by a distinctive style of imagery. There is a natural two-way stylistic development in the work of printmakers, who may choose a specific medium for its characteristic visual qualities, but also find that the techniques feed back ideas for appropriate forms of representation. The highly graphic qualities of prints, such as those described on pages 132–137, can encourage elements of personal style to become more strictly formalised than they usually appear within the looser disciplines of drawing and painting. For professional artists, a strong personal style is useful commercially; and they present themselves with the creative challenge of working out how that style can effectively interpret different elements of a theme, or widely differing subjects.

Printmaking techniques are an interesting area for artists working in a more abstract mode, in that the physical surface qualities of an image are specially important where the subject matter is less immediately accessible to the viewer. In this context, also, strong graphic qualities are worth exploration, the materials and methods of the craft offering unique forms of interpretation that might not occur using other media and processes. But although abstraction tends to focus the viewer's attention on formal and expressive elements of composition, rather than recognisable forms, these purely visual properties are just as essential to the success of representational imagery.

◀ **CAROLE KATCHEN**
DAILY NEWS (ETCHING)

The everyday occurrence makes a memorable image when the artist is alert to both the narrative and pictorial qualities. The postures of these Nigerian women precisely convey how absorbed they are in the gossip of the day. The figures are isolated in the foreground, but given a context with the formal pattern of background silhouettes. The tonal contrast is strongly emphasised, but both dark and light areas contain much subtle, active texture.

◀ **HELEN PEYTON**
BLEACH (LINOCUT)
Washed up on a beach in Devon, the artist became fascinated by this piece of flotsam's journey: was it thrown overboard by a passing ship or had it travelled all the way from Seoul on the tides? The artist likes to incorporate a more painterly approach to printmaking, aiming to soften and abstract the often very deliberate and almost brutal cut of linocut.

▲ **CAROLINE BILSON**
BRIGHTON (LINOCUT)
The recognisable architectural features simplified into striking patterns of black and white are strongly representative of this artist's style and express a sense of place without going into a literal description. Relief-printing media are ideal for this kind of bold, dynamic image, combining crisp contrast with rough, aggressive texture.

▶ **KAZUMASA NAGAI**
I'M HERE (SCREENPRINT)
This is one of a series of prints with a strong conservationist message, using the same basic structure to anchor the stylised representations of the creatures, which take on a powerful symbolic presence. The shapes, colours and patterns are interpreted in a way that produces immediate graphic impact, with each colour printed from a separate screen to maintain the clarity of clean, flat shapes.

I'M HERE
(Save Being and Save World)

▲ **MANDY PAYNE**
EVERYTHING OF VALUE HAS BEEN REMOVED (LITHOGRAPH)
Although representative, this print, inspired by the Brutalist architecture of a council estate in Sheffield, has an abstract feel, thanks to the straight sharp lines and patterns of squares and rectangles. Two stones have been used, with the second stone registered to the first to provide extra tone and depth. Colour was added by block printing different areas using varnished card that had been cut to fit the areas of colour on the print.

◀ PAUL BARTLETT
AFTER VINCENT (LINOCUT)

There is a long tradition of artists learning from or paying homage to past masters by reinterpreting their style and imagery. In this linocut, the direct, graphic qualities are effectively employed to parallel the heavy, swirling brushwork of van Gogh's famous painting. It is printed from one block by the reduction method used for both lino and woodcut prints, re-cutting the design after printing each colour. The ink has been rolled on thickly and overprinting produces some interesting areas of broken colour.

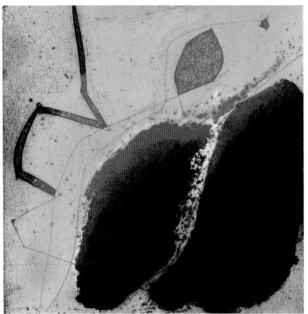

▶ MARY HICK
CAT IN THE GARDEN (LINOCUT)

The artist's love of animals and nature is clear in this decorative, stylised print. The visible cut lines surrounding the cat add a sense of movement to this otherwise sedentary pose. The artist achieves various effects by using tools with different-sized cutting ends. The results can be intricate, but still maintain a look of spontaneity and liveliness.

▶ CATHERINE HEADLEY
EARTH MYSTERIES (COLLAGRAPH)

This abstract imagery is drawn from nature. The collagraph provides the opportunity to combine intaglio line, cut with a scalpel, with areas of relief material, in this case, carborundum (silicon carbide), a fine grit that holds a lot of ink, thus giving rich tonal areas. The plate is inked with orange and red/brown, and then rolled with a fluid, opaque, pale blue ink, which is resisted by the carborundum.

Index

Illustrations are in *italics*.

Acknowledgements

Quarto would like to thank the following for all their help with this project:

The Print Gallery; CCA Galleries; and John and Sheila Elliot in the USA who researched many of the American examples in this book.

Tools and equipment featured throughout were kindly lent by T.N. Lawrence and Son (London and Sussex); L. Cornelissen and Son Ltd (London); George Hall (Sales) Ltd (London).

The following artists helped with the step-by-step sequences in the techniques section:
monoprint: Moira Wills, Judy Martin; linocut: Ian Mowforth, Moira Wills; woodcut: Caroline Bilson; wood engraving: Roland Stringer; collage prints: Judy Martin; screenprinting: Moira Wills; drypoint: Judy Martin; etching: Elisabeth Harden; lithography: Elisabeth Harden.

With special thanks to Morley College in Lambeth, London, whose studios are the backdrop for some of the images in this book.

Every effort has been made to obtain copyright clearance, and we do apologise if any omissions have been made. The author and Quarto would like to thank the following artists for their co-operation.

p2 Vanessa Lubach, www.vanessalubach.co.uk; p10 Helen Peyton, www.helenpeyton.com; p11 *left* Celia Lewis, www.celialewis.co.uk; p11 *right* Anita Reynolds, www.anitareynolds.com; p12 Monoprint: Judy Martin; Screenprint: Moira Wills; Linocut: Ian Mowforth; Drypoint: Juliet Kac; p13 Woodcut: Caroline Bilson; Mezzotint: Philip Coombs; Wood engraving: Roland Stringer; Etching: Elisabeth Harden; Collage blocks: Judy Martin; Lithography: Elisabeth Harden; p18 *right* Elisabeth Harden; p83 Philip Coombs; p109 *top left* Anja Percival, www.anjapercival.com; p109 *bottom right* Louise Bird, www.louisebird.co.uk; p126 Carole Katchen; p127 Vanessa Lubach; p128 Caroline Bilson; p129 Celia Lewis; p130 Pamela Grace, www.pamelagrace.co.uk; p131 Tania Beaumont, www.taniabeaumont.squarespace.com; p132 Ian Scott Massie, www.ianscottmassie.com; p133

Celia Lewis; p134 Liz Myhill, www.lizmyhill.com; p135 Anita Reynolds; p136 Vanessa Lubach; p137 *top left* Jonathan Heale; p137 *bottom right* Helen Peyton; p138 Elisabeth Harden; p139 © L. Roebuck, www.lynneroebuck.uk; p140 David Koster/Wildlife Art Agency; p141 Richard Don Gabriel; p142 Loralie Clemmensen, www.loralieclemmensen.com; p143 *top left* Paul Bartlett; p143 *centre right* Phil Greenwood/CCA Galleries; p144 Kit Boyd, www.kitboyd.com; p145 *top left* Mary Gillett, www.marygillett.co.uk; p145 *bottom centre* Rebecca Owens; p146 Liz Myhill; p147 *left* Ian Scott Massie; p147 *top right* Pip Carpenter/Greenwich Printmakers; p148 Mandy Payne, www.mandypayneart.co.uk; p149 top right Pip Carpenter/Greenwich Printmakers; p149 *bottom* June Ann Sullivan; p150 *centre left* Rebecca Owens; p150 *right* Pamela Grace; p151 Kit Boyd; p152 *top* Ian Mowforth; p152 *bottom* Sally Robson/Greenwich Printmakers; p153 Celia Lewis; p154 Theresa Pateman/Greenwich Printmakers; p155 Helen Peyton; p156 *top centre* Glynn Thomas; p156 *centre left* Susie Perring/Greenwich Printmakers; p156 *bottom right* © L. Roebuck; p157 Linda

Richardson, www.lindarichardson.co.uk; p158 Colin See-Paynton/Wildlife Art Agency; p159 *top left* Carole Katchen; p159 *centre right* Helen Murgatroyd, www.helenmurgatroyd.co.uk; p160 *top left* Peter Strachan/Greenwich Printmakers; p160 *bottom right* Jo Austen, www.jausten.co.uk; p161 Helen Murgatroyd; p162 Jane Daniell, www.janedaniell.info; p163 *top* Kit Boyd; p163 *bottom left* Joy Brand/CCA Galleries; p164 *top left* Donald Harris; p164 *right* Glynn Thomas; p165 Rebecca Owens; p166 Carole Katchen; p167 Helen Peyton; p168 *top left* Caroline Bilson; p168 *top right* Kazumasa Nagai; p169 Mandy Payne; p170 *top left* Paul Bartlett; p170 *bottom centre* Catherine Headley, www.catherineheadley.co.uk; p171 Mary Hick, www.maryhick.com.

Jacket images kindly supplied by Jonathan Heale, Pip Carpenter/Greenwich Printmakers and Sally Robson/Greenwich Printmakers, and with thanks to Morley College, Lambeth, London.